Vector Theory
and the
Plot Structures of
Literature and Drama

by
Cynthia Joyce Clay

ᴀ/ᴄ

Oestara Publishing LLC

Paperback ISBN: 1-59457-778-1
E-book ISBN: 1-59457-814-1

Libraryof Congress Control Number: 2004111971

Publisher: Booksurge LLC
North Charlotte, South Carolina

Oestara Publishing LLC

In Memory of James H. Clay,

my father, and my professor.

And Dedicated to

Guillermo Ramón,

my husband; and

Delight Clay, my mother

Fiction by Cynthia Joyce Clay

Zollocco: A Novel of Another Universe

New Myths of Feminine Divine

The Romance of the Unicorn

Scylla: A Noh Play

Table of Contents

Acknowledgements

First and foremost, I must acknowledge Guillermo Ramón, as he is the one who first recognized that vector theory applies to literature and drama. Kevin Brown kindly supplied me with the bit of history of vector theory given in my introduction. Rolf A. Zwaan, Ph.D. Professor of the Department of Psychology, Florida State University, graciously responded to my e-mail appeal for the psychological term "immersed reader" the concept of which is so important to this work. Raymond T. Anderson tirelessly and efficiently tracked down citations for me that I needed to have double checked. I deeply thank Nia Harper and Dr. Heledd Hayes, the daughters of Gwyn Jones, for allowing me to use gratis Jones' lovely translation of the Welsh poem "Sadness in Spring." Grove/Atalnatic Inc. also did not charge me for the Birch/Keene translation of Li Po's "On the Mountain" which I very much appreciate.

This book began as an article which I prepared for the 8th Annual Conference of the Society for Chaos Theory in Psychology and the Life Sciences, and so thanks are due to Bill Sulis for the premiering of my ideas of "The Application of Vector Theory to Literature and Drama." At that conference I was invited to present the same paper to the 4th International Conference, "Non-Linear World," Languages of Science—Languages of Art in Suzdal, Russia, in June of 1999.

Thanks, then, are due to Igor Yevin for representing the Russian government in inviting me, and the many people at that convention who made the convention such a pleasurable experience for us, especially Natalie, who translated my paper into Russian. Great thanks must also go to the American Embassy in Russia for warning my husband and me that people who have visa problems in Russia end up disappearing and that we must get on the plane back to the USA on the date incorrectly stated on our visas no matter what. Thanks to this timely warning, we did arrive safely back in the USA in spite of the fact that we were not on the Aeroflot flight's itinerary (despite having paid abundantly for the change in ticketing) and that the boarding tickets issued for us by Aeroflot for the New York City to Miami connection turned out to be in other people's names...

In addition to those mentioned above, there have been friends along the way who were happy to see me back and have given me the greatest encouragement such as Pamela Marshall, an award winning composer who is knowledgeable of vector theory and asserts that the emphasis on structure expressed here is how many musicians work; Patricia Harmon, a teacher who is enthusiastic over the educational value of the theories I give here; and Suzanne Oesterriecher, who gleefully throws a book-signing party for me whenever one of my books gets published.

Introduction

Characterization, setting, atmosphere, theme, and plot are the fundamental elements of tales whether the tales be written or performed. Plot is the spine on which all the other elements hang and depend. Nevertheless, plot has remained a rather elusive element, for two major reasons. First, plot has taken so many forms. There are simple plots and complicated plots, dull plots and exciting plots; however, simple plots are not necessarily dull, and complicated plots are not always exciting. The perplexing nature of plot has been difficult to define. So difficult, in fact, that plot has been defined in two entirely different ways, and the two different definitions have frequently been confused as synonymous. The second cause for confusion, then, is that the word *plot* can refer to the storyline of a piece of literature or drama, or it can refer to the architecture of a piece. However, storyline and architecture are not the same. In theater, a distinction between storyline and plot is insisted upon since a play must have shape, dramatic build. Indeed, it is an adage in theater that "plays are not written; they are *wrought*" with an according preference for the *w,r,i,g,h,t* spelling.

Storyline refers to the series of events in a tale, the narrative; *plot* refers to how those events are ordered, structured, or built to create an interesting, exciting, and satisfying experience for the reader or audience. Storyline is a chronicle that requires events which singly and together make cerebral sense and express a passage of time. Plot is a dynamic structuring that gives meaning to different aspects of the piece and creates a single, organically shaped work of art. Plot may make use of metaphors or fragments of images which alone would have no coherent meaning, but, arranged by the writer or playwright, take on meaning. Plot can be composed of events taken out of their time or place, sequenced in such a way as to make those events significant. Film, for instance, has four specialized plotting techniques: the *establishing shot,* which is usually a long shot, shows the interrelationship of details to be shown subsequently in nearer shots (Reisz & Miller 1968, p. 399); *relational editing* (Reisz & Miller, 1968, p. 401) which is an editing of shots to show the associations of ideas between them; *parallel action* which is when the developments of two pieces of action are represented simultaneously by showing a fragment of one then cutting to a fragment of another, and so on back and forth; and the *montage sequence* which is the "quick impressionistic sequence of disconnected images, usually linked by dissolves, superimpostions or wipes, and used to convey passages of time, changes of place, or any other scenes of transit" (Reisz & Miller, p. 112).

While plot has meaning, its meaning may not be cerebral; it may be strictly emotive. Plot may, but need not, be a chronicle—for plot is structure, and so may express how ideas or emotions are created or related. Often storyline in itself has a set structure, but not always. Just as often, a storyline must be given a shape to provide a meaningful experience for reader or audience. A literary work or dramatic piece need not have a storyline, but it must have architecture—shape—to give the reader or audience a satisfying experience. Some pieces are mood pieces, the incidents having no storyline—no events—yet a specific and satisfying experience for the reader or audience is created out of the careful arrangement of those emotion-generating fragments or segments. Haiku is shaped this way, as are some plays like *Waiting for Godot.*

This book examines what literary and dramatic plotting is—what plot is. In drama and literature plot structure has generally been held to fall into two types: episodic and cause-and-effect. Stories of the episodic type are like those exemplified by *The Illiad* and *The Odyssey* which contain a sequence of incidents related only by time and/or theme. Stories of the cause-and-effect type are typified by *Romeo and Juliet* in which each incident causes the next incident: i.e., each incident produces a result which in turn produces another incident. Both kinds of plotting lead to satisfying, aesthetic works. Intuitively it is apparent that as different as these two types of plotting are they must somehow be following a similar structural pattern. A complete aesthetic theory of plotting should clearly describe and define the structural workings of both episodic and cause-and-effect plots to explain what the structural principles are that lie behind both.

Plot is also said to develop excitement through two different means: anticipation and suspense. Literary and dramatic works built through the means of anticipation are those of the ancient Greek theater (i.e. *Oedipus Rex*, *Antigone*) and of the traditional Noh theater in that these plays were originally performed with the assumption that the audience is already familiar with the myths and stories upon which they were based. Since what will happen is known, excitement is generated through the question of "how?" *How* will the events unfold? Hollywood's mysteries and thrillers, on the other hand, generate excitement through suspense. That is, the audience does not know what is going to take place, so excitement is generated through the question of "what?" Again, both suspense and anticipation produce interesting and satisfying works of literature and drama, but the basic structural patterns are so similar that why the plays achieve the effects they do even though they are conceptually so different is unknown.

The elements of plot that have been identified are few in number and have been vaguely defined. Indeed, the tongue-in-cheek definition of structure given regularly in writing magazines is that "a story must have a beginning, a middle, and an end." In schools, students begin their study of plot through learning to spot the climax. Students are taught to do this by being given examples. They are told that the climax will be the most exciting moment that comes near the end of the play. Other than this advice, the student must learn to develop an intuition for finding climaxes through dint of practice. This can be a slow and cumbersome learning process, especially for the student who thinks the whole story is boring and finds no exciting moments in it. Considering that the other major elements of plot (the falling action and the rising action) are defined in relation to the climax, the need for precision in defining plot structure can be appreciated. What exactly are rising action, falling action, and the climax? Since Aristotle, those concerned with dramatic aesthetics have endeavored to answer this question in different ways. So, this book will begin with a summary of the salient aesthetic theories of the theater.

Despite more than two thousand years of thought on the subject, a theory has not been produced within the performing arts or the humanities that defines plot and its elements systematically, logically, and precisely. Nevertheless, such a theory does exist. It is from mathematics, used by engineers to create structures, and known variously as *vector theory*, *vector analysis*, or *vectorial analysis*:

> The first use of what we would call vector analysis was by Simon Stevin in 1586, when he formulated the parallelogram law of forces. Later, Descartes made use of vectors for mechanical and optical reasoning, as did Newton implicitly. Some people say the founder of modern vector analysis was William Hamilton, for his invention of quarternions around 1843, and others say it was Hermann Grassmann, who described a much more general system in 1844 (independently). But most of modern formal vector analysis was developed by Josiah Gibbs and Oliver Heaviside in the late 1800's (Kevin Brown, E-mail, Feb. 10,

1999).

Vector theory was developed to define clearly the activities of forces and other physical quantities. Mathematicians, physicists, and engineers use the word vector to describe what they call physical quantities, or scalors, such as electric charge, time, mass, velocity, displacement, electric field intensity, and force (Jensen & Chenoweth, 1983 pp. 8-10). Thus, the word 'vector' is often used synonymously with the word 'force' because all forces are vectors, though not all vectors are forces (Jensen & Chenoweth, 1983 pp. 8-10).

The premise I am presenting in this book is that the concept of forces in literature and drama is analogous to the concept of forces in physics. In physics, vectors represent the forces that push and pull—that move, propel objects. Vectors will be used analogously to describe how characters, objects, and locations which are the "bodies" of literature and drama reflect the propelling of literary and dramatic "forces." Indeed, the average, educated reader perusing Shakespeare or Cervantes will more readily recognize that what he or she reads is a precise building of forces than that the house within which he or she sits is comprised of carefully structured forces. Almost any fantasy novel will have on its back cover copy that guarantees the reader that "the forces of good and evil" are going to have at in the book. Vector theory "elegantly," as the mathematicians say, describes the workings of plot in literature and drama, and so will give fiction authors and dramatic artists (playwrights, TV and screen writers, actors, designers, choreographers, puppeteers, directors, designers, and TV and film producers) a set of new analytical tools that will help in the creation, revision (including script doctoring and scene rehearsal), and criticism of tales written and performed.

While vector theory is able to answer certain questions more thoroughly than they have been answered before, vector theory supports and supplements traditional forms of criticism. Indeed, in the case of archetypal analysis and metaphorical analysis, vector theory reveals additional levels of pertinence. Since that primary work of aesthetic theory, Aristotle's *Poetics* (which was a theory of drama), literary and dramatic theory have parted company. While salient forms of literary analysis— formalism, archetypal analysis, psychological, feminist, etc.— are known and consistently used by both literary and dramatic artists and theorists, important forms of dramatic theory have been neglected by literary theorists and authors. This is surprising as well as unfortunate since The Method and metaphorical analysis, for example, are very beneficial as instruments of analysis for both drama and literature. Vector theory can undo the growing separation between literary and dramatic theory, and it can and does unite the two.

One of the most important functions of vector analysis in the analysis of literature and drama will be to lay to rest the notion that plot is conflict. This notion has flooded American culture with stories of violence wanting in dimension and has encouraged fiction authors, dramatic artists, readers, and audiences to find conflict in stories that are not about conflict, and so miss the point of the tale. Vector theory yields a real understanding of the workings of plot and this should lead to the greater appreciation of all tales and to the creation of stories of greater scope.

This book will begin with summaries of the major dramatic aesthetic theories, some of which are only noted by dramatic artists. The second chapter will give the basic argument of how vector theory relates to literary and dramatic aesthetics, with subsequent chapters detailing the analogy. The next chapters will relate vector theory in detail with the more important dramatic aesthetic theories, followed by a chapter where four poems are analyzed, line by line, vectorially. The words *drama* and *theater* in this book will be used to refer to most types of theater: the stage, film, TV, mime, "happenings," and puppetry.

***

How was it that I conceived of using vector theory for the study of drama and literature? Frankly, *I* didn't.

One Christmas night, my father, a professor of theater, told my new husband, Guillermo Ramón, and me how a pre-med student had come up to him at the end of class and said, "Isn't it interesting that what *you* [meaning you theater people] study is lies while *we* [meaning we science people] study truth." The student was having difficulty finding correctly the climaxes of plays and was insisting that drama was "all just subjective." My father told us how he tried to explain to the student that it was not subjective, but nothing he said would convince the young man.

Then Guillermo, who had studied engineering in Venezuela and at Ohio State University for four years before changing his major to film, replied, "It is objective, and I can prove it mathematically." And then he gave us a succinct explanation of the forces of drama converging at the same time and place to create a climax. "It's vector theory."

My father and I stared at each other. Guillermo had just solved a millennia-old question. And so, that Yule before the hearth fire, the germ of this book was created.

Chapter One
Traditional Methods of Dramatic Analysis

Since the different types of literary theory are so well known, this book assumes the reader has a basic knowledge of them. Dramatic theory, in contrast, is not universally known. Dramatic artists (playwrights, screenwriters, film producers, directors, actors, designers, choreographers, etc.) use many if not all of the forms of analysis used for literary analysis, but the demands of mounting a production require that alternate forms of analysis be used. Through the march of ages various theoretical approaches to understanding scripts have been advanced. Some theories have withstood the test of time; others have not. Although some theories have fallen into disfavor and/or disuse, they continue to be studied by theater artists because the theories colored the original compositions of the plays and so became part of the scripts' meaning. Further, judicious and restrained use of certain theories still proves fruitful in fleshing out the various aspects of production. Naturally, the theories that have withstood the test of time are of particular importance. Western dramatic artists are usually schooled in all of the theories summarized here (except the Japanese theory of *Yugen*) and usually use these theories as needed and in tandem. This chapter, then, gives a summary of the salient aesthetic theories of drama.

ARISTOTLE'S IDEAS

Regarding plot as structure originated with Aristotle as he discussed tragedy: "...by plot I mean the arrangement of the incidents." Aristotle found that "...most important of all [to tragedy] is the structure of the incidents" (Aristotle, 1970, p.685). He further observed that "...the structural union of the parts being such that, if any one of them is displaced or removed, the whole will be disjointed and disturbed."

Aristotle also made the distinction between episodic plots and cause and effect ones, detesting the former and lauding the latter (Aristotle, p. 689). He felt that "The tragic wonder will then be greater than if they [the incidents] happened of themselves or by accident; for even coincidences are most striking when they have an air of design because pity and fear, which [according to Aristotle] are what tragedy inspires in the audience, is best produced when the events come on us by surprise; and the effect is heightened when, at the same time, they follow cause and effect."

Further, Aristotle discussed the idea of Unity of Plot (Aristotle, p. 687) by which he was probably referring to what now has become a cliché after twenty-three hundred years of repeating—a plot must have "a beginning, a middle, and an end." Inherent to this idea is the notion that "A well constructed plot... must neither begin nor end at haphazard" (Aristotle, p. 687) because "the end must be an organic outgrowth of the beginning, and the beginning occurred because a certain end is in sight."

While examining plot structure, Aristotle determined that "Every tragedy falls into two parts—-Complication and Unraveling or Denouement... By Complication I mean all that extends from the beginning of the action to the part which marks the turning point to good or bad fortune. The Unraveling is that which extends from the beginning of the change to the end." (Aristotle, p. 697) Aristotle (pg. 686) also said that "...the most powerful elements of emotional interest in Tragedy—Peripteia or Reversal of the Situation, and Recognition scenes—are parts of the Plot." A "Reversal of the Situation is a change by which the action veers round to its opposite, subject always to our rule of probability or necessity" (Aristotle, p. 689). "Recognition...is a change from ignorance to knowledge, producing love or hate between the persons destined by the poet for good or bad fortune" (Aristotle, p. 690). Aristotle (pg. 690) felt that "these two parts of the plot turn upon surprises."

A third element of the plots of tragedies was, to Aristotle, the "Scene of Suffering" which is "a destructive or painful action, such as death on the stage, bodily agony, wounds, and the like" (Aristotle, p. 690). From the existence of such scenes Aristotle developed the idea of catharsis when he noted that the dramatic form of "Tragedy...through pity and fear" is a means of "effecting the proper purgation" of these emotions in an audience (Aristotle, p. 685). Aristotle's notions have withstood the test of time, being examined and found valid century after century.

The neoclassical ideas of the Unities, Scribe's Well-Made Play Structure, and even the premise of this book are all derived from the ideas of Aristotle. The ideas of "Reversal and Recognition" were used by Scribe in the formulation of his Well-Made Play Structure. The notions of "Complication" and "Unraveling" also much used by Scribe, are now understood as "rising action" for complication, "climax" for the turning point, and "falling action" for denouement. (The word denouement is still used synonymously with falling action.) The term "complication" is still used for those works that make active use of complications for rising action. The idea of "Unity of Plot" was rethought by the neoclassical theorists who came up with their own interpretation of it. Today, the general thinking favors Aristotle's view that a work must have "a beginning, a middle, and an end." Aristotle's notion of catharsis has moved into current popular understanding of psychology. Aristotle's distinction between cause and effect plots and episodic plots is still the demarcation between plots utilized today. And it is Aristotle's distinction between plot and storyline that led to this book's premise that vectorial analysis presents a universal description of the workings of plot.

THE NEOCLASSICISTS: THE THREE UNITIES And VERISIMILITUDE

The neoclassicists, after studying Aristotle, thought that to be a great work of art a script must (among other things) follow the Three Unities of Time, Place, and Action. By Unity of Time, the neoclassicists meant that all the activities of the play should take only as long as the length of the production itself—a few hours. This proved to be almost impossible to follow, and so a leeway was given in that a full day's activities could be compressed into the few hours of the performance. By Unity of Place, the neoclassicists meant there should only be one locale, one set. By Unity of Action, the neoclassicists meant that there should be a single plot line, no subplots allowed. These ideas were based on concepts of believability, always an important consideration to theater artists. It was felt that audiences could not be expected to believe that more than a day had passed when they had only been sitting there for a few hours. Likewise, since the audience knew they were in one location, they could not be expected to believe that they had moved from place to place. Similarly, the audience could only be expected to believe in one line of action. The adherence to the Three Unities was short lived because it was so difficult to follow that it tended to stifle creativity.

In addition to the Three Unities, the neoclassicists dramatists theorized that plays should have what they called *verisimilitude*, which was comprised of three goals: reality, morality, and generality. To fulfill the goal of reality, the neoclassicists felt that plays should stick to subjects that could actually happen in everyday life, only accepting elements of the fantastic if they were an integral part of a Greek or Roman myth or Biblical tale. To fulfill the goal of morality, the neoclassicists felt that plays should teach a moral lesson and therefore justice should prevail; the wicked should receive their "just desserts." As for the goal of generality, the neoclassicists believed in absolute truths, and so comedy and tragedy should not be mixed; they should be presented in pure form—tragedy untainted by comic moments, comedy free of somber moments. The idea of absolute truths should be expressed in human behavior, and so characters should be types representing the absolutes of human behavior; a beggar should not have noble qualities; a woman should not be manly; a hero should not have faults of character, etc. These ideas, too, were dropped. Later audiences found these elements unrealistic.

The neoclassicists sought to define more closely what Aristotle had articulated. Although they understood that something about time, something about place, and something about action were important, neoclassical theorists' conclusions were wholly shaped by their world view. Since their world-view has not been shared by subsequent centuries or by other cultures, marvelous as the plays they created from these ideas were, their ideas have not been found to be true by audiences not sharing their world view. For this reason, neoclassical theatrical aesthetic notions are only used as a means of understanding neoclassical plays.

THE DELSARTE SYSTEM OF ACTING

A theorist (and actor) of the Romantic period, Francois Delsarte (1811-1871) thought that gestural and vocal expressions of thought and emotion could be categorized and classified scientifically. Delsarte (1893, p. 177) drew up charts of gestures "where we see, for instance, what should be the position of the eye in exaltation, aversion, intense application of the mind, astonishment, etc." Delsarte thought "that man is a triplicate of persons" (1893 p. 172) consisting of "thought, sentiment, and passion" (1893, p. 171) which he termed the "physical, moral, and intellectual persons" (1893, p. 172). (The distinction he made between "sentiment" and "passion" refers to the distinction between the emotions and physical drives.) Gesture and voice must correspond to these aspects of the human condition (1893, p. 52). Thus, "the chest-voice voice [sic] is the expression of the sensitive or vital life, and is the interpreter of all physical emotions. The head voice interprets everything pertaining to scientific and mental phenomena" (1893, p. 52).

The other aspects of vocalization, too, were ascribed three tiers of meaning. Further, the head, torso, limbs, and hands were each divided into three zones which have specific meaning. For instance, the higher regions of the head and torso were related to the intellect; their mid-sections related to feelings; and their lower regions were related to the basic drives, the passions. The limbs, the wrists and feet (Delsarte, 1893, p. 111) were related to the mind; the elbows and knees to the feelings; and the thighs and shoulders to the basic drives. By following this system of categorization the performer could establish characterization through movement and voice. Villains were portrayed by making use of gestures and vocal patterns of the various "physical" zones; women from the zones of sentiment (there being just one type of woman, naturally); and the rest of the male roles from the zones most clearly related to their characters.

During Delsarte's time characterization was frequently the driving force within scripts because plays were written as "vehicles" to support and show off the talents of a specific actor. The action sprung from the behavior of the character when he or she was set in certain circumstances. This being the case, a dramatic theory that emphasized characterization was much appreciated. Delsarte's theory explained that there were certain types of characters who would act in certain ways and who could be expected to engage in certain types of activities. Of course, a character type need not be pure—each of the three qualities could form a character's personality. Nevertheless, one type of quality would be the dominant trait. Although Delsarte's theory was (and still is) practiced by actors for movement and voice, Delsarte's followers saw it also as a means of analyzing literature.

The theory that acting can be categorized and charted as a science had nearly fallen by the wayside, the set of choices of movement and interpretation being much too narrow for modern understanding of human behavior. However, some theatrical artists have found that discreet touches of the Delsarte System help to establish character for an audience on an immediate, gut level. Many leading theater artists who specialize in movement (dancers, mimes, and movitions) have, since Delsarte's time, been trained in his theories (http://www.pitt.eu/~sillis/dance/ruth. htm; Ross Clay, personal conversation, June 11, 2001). Indeed, a new theater company in New York City has arisen, garnering many awards. The Interborough Repertory Theater has as a mission the creation of a more physical form of drama through the blending of Delsarte's system of movement with American Sign Language, a theater form called Del-Sign (http://bdstudios.com/IRTonline.html). Delsarte's aesthetic system was designed around the needs of the actors' instrument (body and voice), not on plotting. Nevertheless, it did address structure in that it identified typical forces in the plays of the day. Intellect, sentiment, and passion were basically forces of personality that responded to each other and to situations for better or worse.

THE WELL-MADE PLAY STRUCTURE

The Well-Made Play Structure was a formula for writing plays invented by French playwright Eugene Scribe (1701-1861). Scribe used the Well-Made Play structure to compose more than three hundred plays that met with popular success. The Well-Made Play structure is built around a cause-and-effect plot that uses misunderstandings and withheld information as devices to create suspense. Often this information takes the form of a secret which the audience knows but the characters do not. The play begins with an exposition, followed by a build of incidents, with the protagonist suffering various mishaps or reversals of fortune. These incidents and reversals continue, intensifying the plot, until a startling revelation (usually given in a letter) causes a reversal in the form of a victim, or powerless character, suddenly acquiring power or strength. Often the powerless character is the protagonist who was made powerless by previous reversals of fortune. Incidents continue to build, and suspense is created by misunderstandings and the mystery of the withheld information. The climax is reached when a vital piece of information is revealed, and a logical and tidy working out of the various complications finishes the play. Plays constructed around the principles of the Well-Made Play structure almost always ended with a happy ending, but they need not do so to be in keeping with the formula.

Although largely considered to be a contrived, hackneyed formula which all too often produces scripts devoid of depth of character, Ibsen did make use of the Well-Made Play structure for his masterpiece *Ghosts*. However, while audiences had come to expect happy endings from the Well-Made Play structure, Ibsen did not give them one with *Ghosts*. (That combined with the subject matter—venereal disease—caused public outcry against *Ghosts*.) Use of the Well-Made Play structure is now rare, but it has not ceased. The exquisite film *Babette's Feast* follows the Well-Made Play structure precisely. The fact that Scribe's formula for constructing scripts has consistently yielded plays of popular appeal as well as dramatic pieces of great richness means that it is an important contribution to aesthetic theory.

YUGEN

Yugen is the aesthetic principle behind much of Japanese art, particularly the Noh drama. *Yugen* refers to the quality of mystery and profundity that cannot be directly expressed in words (Tsunoda, De Bary, & Keene, 1958). The Noh actor, to be a master, is to imbue his performance with *Yugen*, to carry his performance beyond mere representation into the realm of transcendence. The actor is to do this through subtlety and restraint in his performance. *Yugen* is to be achieved, according to the most famous playwright-actor of the Noh, Seami (1363-1443), through beauty and gentleness of form. *Yugen* is to be found in elegance of costuming, grace of language and mastery of educated speech, in the smooth and sensitive flow of movement in beautiful music, in flawless technique and serenity of movement in dance, and in maintaining beauty of effect when displaying the emotions of one's character (Seami, trans. Tsunoda et al, 1958). Thus Seami sought "to make of the Noh a symbolic theatre, in which the most important actions were not represented but suggested" (Tsunoda, et al. 1958).

Since in Noh drama the climax is traditionally in the form of a dance, these qualities are an intrinsic aspect of the Noh play, not a mere veneer. *Yugen* describes how the structure is to be expressed, not what structure the plot follows. *Yugen*, as a quality, relates more to the tone and meaning of a play or a story rather than to a tale's architecture. While an important contribution to theatrical aesthetic theory, the concept of *Yugen* is not about plot, but about the type of reality being dramatically expressed.

THE TRAGIC FLAW

Used most often to describe Shakespeare's plays and classical drama, this theory holds that a character has one ruling quality which is the essence of his or her being and determines his or her destiny. This immutable quality propels him or her to act in certain ways at all times and so eventually brings the character to his or her doom. Thus, Brutus is driven to his doom by his sense of honor, Hamlet by his need to find the truth before he acts, and Macbeth by his ambition. This theory is still in use. Indeed, it is often taught to high school students as they study Shakespeare.

THEATER OF CRUELTY

Antoin Artaud developed a theatrical aesthetic, Theater of Cruelty, which he described in his book, *The Theater and Its Double* (Artaud, 1958). Suffering from mental illness, troubled by what he felt was an unhealthy society, and impressed by the cathartic effects of Indian rituals of the Americas which he had witnessed, Artaud felt the theater should be a form of shock treatment that would frighten and shock audience members out of unhealthy forms of social compliance and relieve or cure them of mental illness. Theater should take its place with ritual as a therapeutic experience. As such, theater should help the audience break from preconceived ways through performances that are comprised of disjointed, unrelated, alarming scenes and happenings, and jolting, unexpected, and frightening screams and noises. By jolting the audience away from the expected, and startling and frightening them with cacophonies, the theater should force the audience members to get back in touch with their real feelings and be returned to a natural state of mental health.

Artaud's theatrical aesthetic was lauded in his own time by the avant-garde theater, and his Theater of Cruelty makes reappearances. Theater of Cruelty appeared again as part of the protest theater during the Vietnam War. During the sixties and seventies in the United States, when dissidents felt strongly that American society was becoming unhealthily, perhaps dangerously ossified, protest theater used Artaud's ideas to shake up society, implicitly present in the form of the audience. Audiences do throng to Theater of Cruelty performances, and go away feeling satisfied, if disturbed and puzzled, by the experience.

Since the aim of Theater of Cruelty is to be cathartically therapeutic, the disjointedness and shocks are carefully structured and paced to make them truly disjointed and shocking, and built through pacing and intensity to really make the audience feel it has become unhinged. Although plot usually is structured to make an audience feel something is all of a whole, if the point is to make the audience feel split, then the plot structure has to be as carefully conceived as in a non-avant-garde production. Theater of Cruelty can be looked at as plotting used to disassemble the audience's point of view, rather than assembling the audience's point of view. Theater of Cruelty is one of the very few forms of avant-garde theater that has proved artistically viable, has withstood the test of time, and manages to remain ever avant-garde.

CONFLICT THEORY

The theory of conflict, the currently prevailing idea of plotting, was first conceptualized by Georg Hegel (Lawson, 1960, p. 37) and brought into modern form by Ferdinand Brunetiere (Lawson, 1960, p. 59). Hegel held that the principle of "tragic conflict" was "The moving force in dramatic action: the action is driven forward by the unstable equilibrium between man's will and his environment—the wills of other men, the forces of society and of nature" (Lawson, p. 37). Brunetiere developed this into the "law of conflict" stating that "Drama is the representation of the will of man in conflict with the mysterious powers or natural forces which limit and belittle us; it is one of us thrown living upon the stage, there to struggle against fatality, against social law, against one of his fellow mortals, against himself, if need be, against the ambitions, the interest, the prejudices, the folly, the malevolence of those who surround him" (Lawson, p. 59). Thus, conflict theory holds that a struggle between opposing components of the dramatic or literary piece is the essence of plot construction. Unlike the Delsarte System and The Method, conflict theory holds that it is the oppositional relationship between the characters that is important, rather than who the characters are or what they do; thus, conflict theory presumes drama and literature to be a dynamic—an interactive system involving conflicting forces. The clash of impulses, desires, or goals; the sharp disagreement between interests or ideologies; the contention over motivations, interests, or viewpoints; and the strife between contending desires, interests, or objectives are regarded as the fundamental basis for creating and increasing dramatic tension in dramatic and literary works. The form most commonly taken, therefore, is that the protagonist and the antagonist are fighting about something either figuratively (often) or literally (usually). However, according to the theory, the opposing components need not necessarily consist of characters even though most proponents of Conflict understand Conflict as occurring between the characters.

The components of Conflict can also be thematic or symbolic elements which are in conflict. Whatever the components consist of, each must be paired with a contender. To some adherents of the theory of conflict, strife in its physical form of aggression is viewed as integral to plot construction in drama. Thus, the antagonist is viewed as a hostile opponent to the protagonist's motives and/or objectives. Regardless of whether the struggle is presented in a literal or figurative manner, the moment of greatest struggle must be, in the theory of conflict, the climax. It must be the climax because it should be the final, determining struggle. Since it is considered that the more pairings of struggling elements there are the more exciting the plot will be, the most exciting climax consists of the moment when a vast number of opposing pairings engages all at once in a vigorous struggle. This can, and often does, take the form of two huge parties of characters engaging in a vigorous struggle (as in a battle), or it can take the form of two small parties of characters who embody numerous elements engaging in a literal or figurative fray.

For instance, Superman is not just the element of the character himself; he is also the elements of "Truth, Justice, and the American Way," which are massive elements in themselves. The falling action of a piece then shows whether the antagonist or protagonist (or neither) elements have prevailed. The falling action also finishes any minor points of struggle that might still be extant. There is no doubt that the theory of conflict has been extremely useful, not only in the interpretation of dramatic and literary pieces but in the construction of them as well. It may well be argued that no theory to date has yielded a more productive system of plot interpretation or construction.

However, the theory of conflict is not completely universal in that some literary and dramatic pieces do not lend themselves easily to this form of interpretation, and some do not lend themselves to it at all. Another shortcoming of conflict theory is that as a quick and easy system of plot creation it promotes physical spectacle more often than it does artistic pieces of profundity. Moreover, the theory of conflict is also responsible for a tendency of adherents to rely on violence to maintain reader or audience interest. Conflict theory has so strong a holding in current literary and dramatic aesthetics that plot is often defined as conflict. Nevertheless, conflict theory tends to produce shallow, violent films and books, and also tends to foster interpretations of contention in stories that are not about contention. These shortcomings, and why conflict theory should be abandoned, are delved into in a later chapter.

THE METHOD

Originated by the Russian actor Constantin Stanislavsky, The Method is the primary theory of the theater in the United States today. It is also prevalent in the former Soviet Union and in China. The Method provides dramatic artists with a system of analyzing plays for theatrical interpretation. It also provides a means for allowing that interpretation to be performed. Those means consist chiefly of acting techniques for focusing concentration and building fresh emotions as required by the script. As technical aspects of the actor's art, that part of The Method need not be elaborated upon in this book. Thus, only The Method's system of analyzing scripts will be discussed here. What follows, then, is a summary of The Method's analytical methodology.

First, each character is examined for identity, or character type—old man, wife, angry young man, young girl, etc., because the actor must have some general idea of who his or her character is. Once this is established, the actor proceeds to think of his or her character in the first person in order to start the humanizing process. Next, the dramatic artist determines the character's objective—that is, what it is the character wants. This is important because the objective provides the actor with a through-line. A through-line is what remains more or less consistent for the character from scene to scene. It is the skeleton on which the actor's performance is built. The objective is then stated as an action verb in the infinitive form following the assertion "I want"; for example, "I want to ruin so-and-so." Action verbs are needed because states of being cannot be acted out. A character's objective is established for the play as a whole and also for every single scene within the play. Each scene may have an objective which is slightly different from but still relates to the overall objective. For instance, Hamlet wants to avenge his father's death, but he also wants to prove his uncle's guilt (the play within the play scene, Act IV) and to lash out at Ophelia (the returning of love-tokens scene, Act III, i).

How the character accomplishes his or her objective is also determined. Usually, the character has to try several different means of acquiring his objective—otherwise the play would end in the first scene. A character may try several different tactics within each scene. For instance, if the overall objective is "I want to kill so and so," then different means of killing so and so are entertained. Often the different strategies of accomplishing the overall objective create the variations on the objective, such as "I want to connive you into killing so and so."

The dramatic artist will also study the script to find the character's motivation—why the character does what he does. The character's motivation or motivations (he can have different ones at different times) are considered crucial to find because the motivation is a major element of what allows the audience to "suspend disbelief" to find the character and his actions believable. Since audiences require the theatrical piece to be believable, it is assumed that the character always has a reason for doing what he or she does.

Not only does the character have a motivation, he has a life "between scenes." That is, the character was some place doing and thinking something prior to what the audience sees that led him or her to the onstage action. The actor is obliged to imagine what that off-stage life is as suggested by the script. (What other characters report about the character is one factor used to construct an off-stage life for the character.) Further, what happens in the scene also will result in the character going somewhere "off-stage" to do something else. This, too, must be decided upon by the actor from hints in the script. Imagining a character's off-stage life enables the actor to give his or her performance continuity, and if there are flaws in the script, mend those flaws so they are not troublesome to the audience.

Each time there is a change in the objective, a change in tactic, or a change in the character's motivation a demarcation is made in the script (usually by a line) and also in the eventual performance either by a pause, a pause accompanied by a change of the actor's position on stage, or some other signal visual effect. Thus, blocks or sections in the script are noted, and these blocks are referred to as "beats" or "motivational units." The dramatic artist also analyzes who is "driving the scene." Usually, one character is in control. If control passes from one character to another, this is also marked as a beat change, and a significant one at that. In film, significant beat changes are often denoted by music.

Since a character has an off-stage life, a motivation, and an objective, the actor is constantly thinking about them as he or she performs. The actor thinks about them as if they are the qualities of his or her own life (in the first person) and these thoughts affect the actor's feelings. This undercurrent of thought and feeling is known as "subtext" and gives life and dimension to the actor's performance and added dramatic tension to the production as a whole.

Each individual Method actor does this close scrutiny of a script for his or her own character.

The director also does it, but for every single character within the play. He must, after all, as he or she coordinates all the individual performances. The designers also examine the script in this way because off-stage lives, motivations, and objectives affect lighting changes, indicate what props are needed, and govern costuming needs. Furthermore, even before production begins, when selecting works of literature for translation into a dramatic piece, theatrical artists look for these basic elements of character types—off-stage life, objectives, and motivations to determine whether the story is playable. This rigorous form of script analysis has proven to be a highly effective as well as an intellectually satisfying way of constructing both interpretations of scripts and the scripts themselves. The questions "Who am I and what do I want?" posed by Method dramatic artists to better understand and interpret scripts, can also be used fruitfully by those who study and create works of literature. The relationship that this form of analysis has to plotting is that since each character has an objective that is actively pursued, the events of the production are created by the characters as a means towards goals. This means that the climax is the moment when the main characters either accomplish their primary aims (their objectives) or fail.

METAPHORICAL ANALYSIS

Besides engaging in a Method analysis and an analysis of the conflict, theatrical artists, especially directors, designers, and television producers, engage in what will here be called metaphorical analysis. Even if an analysis of the script's conflict or a Method analysis is not done (English actors tend not to follow The Method), a metaphorical analysis is considered crucial to those interested in creating a work of art.

In metaphorical analysis, dramatic artists study:

1.Sources other than the script such as:

a) The cultural context of the script, such as habits of dress, rules of etiquette, social customs, and topical events;

b) The prevailing paradigm and the prevailing aesthetic theory of the day;

c) The physical form of the theater, such as whether the theater was outdoor or indoor, and if indoor, what mechanical devices or lighting equipment was used;

d) the acting conventions of the day such as the use of the fourth wall, the use of masks, the use of stylized movement, ensemble acting or the star system

e) The canon of the day, including fairy tales and parables, and especially other works by the same playwright;

f) The specific audience for which the script was intended;

g) The actors (if any) for whom the roles were specifically written;

2.The script itself in terms of:

a) Its need for adherence to the items listed above;

b) What new conventions the script lends itself to;

c) What visual elements are stressed?

d) What auditory elements are stressed?

e) What analogies are being drawn?

f) What symbolic motifs are stressed?

g) What metaphors are repeatedly created?

Dramatic artists routinely analyze each of these items to help choose a central, metaphorical image for the production of a script. To those in the arts and humanities, the difference between a metaphor and an analogy is quite apparent, but for those mathematicians and physicists who tend to think of those words as interchangeable, let me clarify the distinction. An analogy is when correspondences and similarities exist between things that are otherwise dissimilar. A metaphor is when an emotional tie, relationship, or similarity is made between things, regardless of whether the things bear any real correspondences. The analogy is a factual comparison; the metaphor is an emotional comparison.

The purpose of the analogy is to give a clearer understanding of one thing by reference to another already understood. The purpose of the metaphor is to enlarge, to make greater and more encompassing the meaning of one thing by associating it with something else. Metaphors need to evoke emotional ties between things because this is how many stories are created with one story; how layers of meaning are built into a single plot. A metaphorical image, then, is an emotion-laden visual representation that connects all the different meanings of the script into a single, unified, dynamic statement. This "production concept" as it is often called, is created to give organic cohesiveness to every aspect of the production from the general floor plan of the set to the specific delivery of actors' lines. Set design, costume design, lighting designs, acting styles will all reflect the metaphorical image chosen.

For instance, James Clay, co-author of *The Theatrical Image,* asked one of his Introduction to the Theater classes at Brandeis University to come up with production concepts for the play *The Glass Menagerie.* One student developed the idea of ice sculptures in an old, dirty oven. The cool blues suggested by the image of the ice sculptures melting away in the heat of an oven stained orange and brown with use provide the color schemes for contrasts between Laura and her glass animals and the relentless, boxed-in heat of the apartment and the mother's demands. Laura's behavior is also suggested by the image, sweetly and refreshingly cool, as is the mother's, behavior marked by a temper that simmers, bakes, and chars all those within its confines. Also, the image clearly reflects what will happen; ice sculptures can do nothing but melt inside of an oven.

An example of a professional production concept would be Laurence Olivier's utilization of Freud's theory of the Oedipus complex—a young man in love with his own mother—to define and shape his production of *Hamlet* (Clay and Krempel, 1967, p. 247-254). The production concept, which is chosen by the director, gives the point of view of the material being presented for performance. This is particularly important for period pieces that no longer have the automatic commands of interest topicality or shared world view. Clay and Krempel (personal conversations Dec. 1979) and many theater artists feel that "just doing the play" with no unifying concept makes for nothing but a "boring" production. A production can be in all ways technically proficient, but without a point of view, without a central, unifying metaphorical image, the production will strike its audience as soulless.

To find the essence, the soul of a piece, metaphorical analysis leads dramatic artists to think about a script metaphorically—to think of the emotional connections otherwise unrelated things evoke. The central question of metaphorical analysis is "What is this play like?" with the "like" meaning "feel like." This metaphorical thinking is "the central principle of theatrical meaning and its interpretation" (Clay & Krempel, 1967, p. 262).

Since the theatrical image, the metaphorical image, is central to the production's meaning, the image chosen must truthfully reflect the emotional impact of the script. The image must render appropriate choices for colors, shapes, lights, sounds, and movements; and the image must also suggest the ultimate change that is going to occur in the play. An ultimate change, or a transformation, is assumed to be part of every production that is a work of art, and the transformation occurs at the climax. The theatrical image must give the moment of climax the greatest metaphorical meaning. Thus, in the student's concept, the ice sculptures will be distorted and destroyed by melting when the heat of the oven is on full blast. In

Olivier's production, the audience understands that an Oedipus complex is a diseased, shadowy passage in the mind and can lead to nothing but the destruction of Hamlet and everyone he loves.

The production concept works to clarify the plot's shape by accentuating and defining pivotal elements and moments. It is the principle means of elucidating the plot because the aspects of the piece that has to do with the work's deeper meanings are given their due significance by the metaphorical image, and aspects that are less weighty are accordingly given less relevance. By organically unifying the elements of a production, the central, metaphorical image gives the production meaning, beauty, and life. Theatrical artists naturally look at short stories, novels, and poems for their overriding metaphorical statements; indeed the metaphor presented by a novel or short story is often the source of inspiration for its adaptation into a play or film.

The Poetics, the Three Unities and Verisimilitude, the Well-Made Play, the Delsarte Theory of Acting, Theater of Cruelty, Conflict, The Method, and Metaphorical Analysis are Western aesthetic theories of the theater. Of the Western theories, only neoclassical ideas have been totally discredited and are only studied for the relevance to the plays they produced.

Yugen, as an aesthetic theory of the East, is unknown and therefore unused by Westerners although the Noh theater, the theater form about which Seami was concerned, has endured longer than any style of Western theater and is appreciated as much today as it was in the 1400's. However, when considering the nature of plot, *Yugen* must be crossed from the list because it is not concerned with plot construction.

The Three Unities and Verisimilitude must be crossed from the list, too, because the Unities are stultifying, and Verisimilitude is unbelievable for theatrical artists and audiences alike. Theater of Cruelty, as performance to achieve the breaking down of harmful societal conditioning is concerned with plot construction—theatrical structures that create transformation through surprise and shock. Aristotle's ideas provide a basic understanding of plotting, as well as a framework for the Well-Made Play structure. The Method and the Delsarte Theory of Oratory point up the relevance of characterization to plotting and resonate well with both the Well-Made Play structure and Aristotle's ideas. Conflict theory provides a simple, straightforward way of approaching the more complicated plots Aristotle and Scribe described and also simplifies both The Method's approach towards characterization and the already simple, categorized Delsarte System of characterization. Metaphorical analysis gives dimension to and unifies all of the former.

Although these forms of analysis can be synthesized together quite well, there is still the problem that plot has not to date been clearly defined. Saying a plot has a beginning, middle, and end, is not saying much of anything. Aristotle himself, who first defined fallacies, would cheerfully admit that saying the rising action is the part leading up to and including the climax; the denouement is the part after and including the climax, and the climax is the part after the rising action and before the falling action, is nothing more than a tautology. Likewise, giving a long list of types of events, an index, as the Well-Made Play structure does, is not giving a definition of plot. The idea inherent in the Delsarte System that plot is defined by a character-type set in a situation is too vague and open-ended. The Method's motivations and objectives are useful but still lacking in defining plot. Saying that plot is conflict is so limited a definition as to corrupt the arts of storytelling into mere recounts of acts of aggression. Metaphorical analysis can provide us with an emotional understanding of plotting, but an analogy is needed for an objectively understood definition. In the next chapter, then, an objective definition of plot is given; a definition broad enough to encompass all of the hard-won theatrical aesthetic theories, but specific enough to truly describe how plots are structured.

Vector theory can encompass these aesthetic theories that have been found to be "workable" (e.g. consistently helpful in providing interpretations that meet the demands of performance) and so is beneficial to literary and theatrical artists and theorists and yields a truly universal theory of plot. Vector theory and its compatibility with the already existing dramatic theories form the basis of the rest of the book.

Chapter Two

Vector Theory and Its Application to Drama and Literature

It has long been supposed that there is an underlying order to works of literature and drama, but this order has not been precisely described. Therefore, dramatic artists are accustomed to basing their work on intuition. For instance, they learn to quickly and easily spot a climax; a skill that some undergraduates never learn. Likewise, theatrical artists learn to sense what lines in a play will receive laughter and which require some kind of a movement, knowing the movement will bring out a specific emotional meaning to the line.

There are times during rehearsal when the director will tell the actors to "pick up the pace" or "milk it." The former means to move and say lines more quickly; the latter means to go slowly and fully reveal all the levels of emotion of a passage of the script. However, by the fortieth or fiftieth rehearsal, nothing is funny; intuition refuses to assert itself; and the actors and director know they must rely on the fact that when they first read the script it was funny. Dress rehearsal is normally a disaster. No one can remember lines or blocking, the timing is all wrong, and everything the director has told the actors to do they forget to do. Nevertheless, the very next night, the audience laughs when the actors think they should; indeed, an enthralling evening of theater takes place, leaving the audience satisfied, happy, and feeling that this was a special evening in their lives. If the audience does not feel this way, the show closes and the dramatic artists are out of work maybe for years.

Such a situation would make anyone a little high strung. So, if there were a precise way to describe plot, if the workings of plot could be analyzed with as much definition as the trajectories of shooting stars, it would help immeasurably.

But wait! The sudden brilliance of the meteor, its flaming path across the sky, its gradual yet beautiful extinguishing as it passes overhead is precisely understood, and can, and often is, plotted on a graph. The force of the speeding meteor meets the resisting force of the earth's atmosphere. The force of friction burns away some of the meteor and particles within the atmosphere collide with particles of the meteor and the forces of the collision wreak havoc. The forces are charted, and the physicists know exactly what happened to the meteor and why because they understand the mathematics of forces. This mathematics of forces is variously called vectorial analysis, vector analysis, or vector theory.

Vectors are abstract representations of properties underlying effects. In physics and engineering, vectors represent the forces that push and pull—that move, propel objects. Engineers, who build roads and buildings just as costumers build costumes, set designers build sets, actors build characters, and playwrights build suspense, understand vectors this way: "The graphical representation of a vector quantity in its proper magnitude, direction, and sense is called a vector" The "...'direction' refers to both parallelism and orientation" (Jensen and Chenoweth, 1983, p. 8). The direction is the representation of the pathway or course the object follows. The "...'sense' of a vector" (Pettofrezzo, 1966, p. 4) "is indicated by the way it acts...upward or downward, to the right or to the left..." and "forces acting upward or to the right are positive, and forces acting downward or to the left are negative." (Jensen & Chenoweth, 1983, p. 26). It is to be noted that "Some...prefer to include the sense of a force within the meaning of the term direction. However, in most problems involving the solution of an unknown force, its direction is known but its magnitude and sense are unknown. Preferably, therefore, a distinction is drawn between direction and sense" (Jensen & Chenoweth, 1983, p. 8). The magnitude is a weight (Jensen & Chenoweth, 1983, p. 8), "length of the line" (Chen-To Tai, 1992, p. 1), or, in general terms, an amount. "Forces arise from the direct action of two bodies in contact with one another or from the 'action at a distance' of one body upon another..." (Mase, 1998, p. 367) and then "The resultant of several forces acting at a point is a force which will produce the same effects as all the individual forces acting together" (Avallone and Baumeister, 1996, p. 3-3). Therefore, vectors can be added to (Thrall and Tornheim, 1957, p. 2) and subtracted from each other (Pettofrezzo, 1966, p. 5-7).

A last principle is an extension of this idea of forces causing bodies to make contact with each other: "When the action lines of all the forces of a system intersect at a common point, the system is said to be concurrent." (Jensen & Chenoweth, 1983, p. 10) "Thus, the resultant of a concurrent force system is a single force acting at the point of concurrency, and being the vector sum of the individual forces" (Mase, 1998, p. 368). When two bodies make contact, the sense of the new force will be that of whichever force of the two bodies had the greater magnitude. The magnitude will be the sum (in the case of same-sense vectors) or difference (in the case of different-sense vectors), and a new direction will be established as a consequence of the bodies' contact. When several bodies make contact, the same-sense vectors will be added and the sum of the negative and the sum of the positive will then be added to form the resultant. Colliding bodies may also make direct impact or an oblique impact (Jensen and Chenoweth, 1983, p. 414). An oblique impact can be more easily understood as a glancing blow. A direct impact usually causes the destruction of the bodies.

To cast some of these concepts in the common parlance, the word "convergence" will be used to refer to the action lines of forces intersecting. That is, when bodies conveying forces meet at the same time and place, the forces will be said to be "converging." Once the forces propelling the bodies have converged they will be said to have "transformed" since a new force is created out of the forces' converging. The resulting force will be frequently referred to as the "transformed" force. It is to be stressed that the term "transform" is to be taken in its Standard English meaning. Scientists tend to use the words "change" and "transform" interchangeably to mean something can be altered into something else and then made to revert back to its original form. However, in literary and dramatic theory, indeed, in Standard English, only the word "change" means this. "Transform" means that once it has been altered into something else it can not be reverted back; the alteration is permanent.

The words *sense* and *direction* also are used differently by scientists, using "direction" not in the way of common parlance to indicate how it is moving (cardinal directions, clockwise/counter clockwise, up/down, etc.) but to mean the course-way itself, and using *sense* not to mean "perceive" or "be aware of" but to mean, well direction. (Since scientists are using the word *transform* to mean merely *change*; those of them studying dynamic systems are facing the difficulty of not having a word to mean transform, so *bifurcation* is being used in dynamic systems to say that one state has changed permanently into another state. The word *bifurcation* actually means that something has split into two separate things, and this is how that word is used in engineering and the rest of the science, so the use of *bifurcation* to mean transform is an inaccurate use of the word. We can only hope that in the future theoretical scientists will enlist the aide of linguists before they go about creating terms.) In this book, *metaphor*, *transformation*, and *converge* will be used instead of the mathematical terms for clarity, but *sense* and *direction* will be used in the way of mathematics, since the analytical method of the mathematics is the system under discussion.

Vector theory is an important contribution to the comprehension of forces, for several reasons. Vector theory precisely defines forces as (a) having a direction (moving along a pathway); (b) having positive sense (moving up, to the right, or clockwise) or having negative sense (moving down, to the left, or counterclockwise); and (c) being quantifiable in some way. Vector theory further gives a specific description of the action lines of forces intersecting (converging) and changing as a result (transforming). In engineering, vectors are understood to propel and move bodies, and to make bodies resist being moved. Vectors, as abstract representations of forces, can be used analogously to describe how characters, objects, and locations, which are the "bodies" of literature and drama, reflect the propelling of literary and dramatic "forces."

That is, when the characters, settings, and objects of fiction and drama are regarded as conveying forces, they can be described as conveying vectors having sense, direction, and magnitude. The rising action, the climax, and the falling action can be understood in terms of a structured set of vectorial convergences and resultants just as the engineers conceive of a building as a structured set of vectorial convergences. Vector theory parallels basic notions already held in dramatic aesthetics. These basic dramatic ideas matched with their counterparts from vector theory are:

1. A story has "movement" in that the major elements of the story seem propelled along a specific course. That forces move along a course-way is the concept of *direction* in vector theory.

2. The elements of a story align themselves into countering qualities which are usually conceived as the protagonistic forces against antagonistic forces, but such forces need not be "good" and "bad"—they can be any thematic

elements that are of an opposite or opposing nature. In vector theory this same principle is defined as sense and the forces are referred to as either positive or negative.

3.Characters, settings, and props have abilities or powers that allow them to exert influence on or move each other; and some characters, settings, and props have more ability or power than others. This idea matches directly vector theory's notion of magnitude.

4.The characters, props, and settings meet or interact, causing rising action. When the protagonistic elements meet with each other, they combine their strengths. When the antagonistic elements meet with each other, they combine their strengths. When protagonistic and antagonistic elements meet or interact, whichever set of elements is more powerful triumphs; if they are equally powerful, they obliterate each other. This, too, matches directly with vectorial analysis. Vectors can be added together, and when different sense vectors converge, the vector of the greater magnitude is the one that remains extant.

5.The most exciting moment of the story or play, coming somewhere close to the end, is the climax. The climax usually consists of the protagonist and the antagonist having one, big, final confrontation. After the climax it is necessary to have falling action (why is not known in aesthetics), and the achieving of the climax and falling action make the work a complete, dramatic structure. In vector theory, when all the vectors converge (all the action lines of the forces intersect) at the same time and place, the system is concurrent—the edifice is completed (Jensen & Chenoweth, 1983, p. 10).

6.The triumphing character, prop, or even

setting is not who it was at the beginning of the story; it is transformed in some fundamental way. This is directly analogous to "The resultant of a concurrent force system is a single force comprised of all the forces of the system" (Jensen & Chenoweth, 1983, p. 10) (Mase, 1998, p. 368). That is, according to vector theory, the converging of all the forces turns the remaining vector into a new force.

To find what the forces are in literature and drama, the basic principles of statics provide a highly revealing analogy. In statics it is said that forces "can be exerted only through the action of one physical body on another, either in contact or at a distance." Also forces can resist each other (Jensen & Chenoweth, 1983, p. 7). Thus, engineers have a simple method of determining vectors. They represent any movement and any resistance to movement as a vector (G. Ramon, personal conversations, June 1998, July 1999).

The definition from statics and the engineer's guideline can easily be applied to literature and drama for a preliminary search for vectors. For literature and drama the analogy of a vector can be extended a bit to encompass anything conveying a vector that has being transported as part of its nature. Further, using the analogy of vectors allows for the concept of bodies acting at a distance from each other to lead to another way of determining what constitutes a force in literature. Anything that draws things to it or into itself is also acting as a force. For literature and drama, this means that any character, location, or object that can move, be transported, or draw things to itself should be regarded as a conveying force.

However, a bit of further clarification is needed. It is not the character, object, or location but the characteristics of the character, object, or location that are vectors. For instance, a car can be represented as its acceleration vector. One thinks of the car as the acceleration because it is an accelerating vehicle, but the acceleration is not really the car. Besides the acceleration, there may be many other vectors that are part of what the car is doing. As the car moves, there are friction forces between the car and the road, between the car and the air, and between the different moving and stationary parts that form the car. Nevertheless, in analyzing the car the vectors are only included if they are relevant to the wanted results.

This idea of relevancy is as important to analyzing literature and drama as it is to engineering problems. A way of looking at relevancy in literature and drama is whether the element contributes to a greater understanding of character and/or theme; whether it assists in moving the plot along (creates movement, "picks up the pace," or causes more incidents to occur); or whether it helps to create atmosphere.

To return to the analogy, in most pieces of literature and drama, these results will usually be affected by vectors working through three forms: characters, objects, or locations. Further, in literature and drama, relevancy, or contributing to wanted results, takes the form of whether the character, object, or location conveys meaning. The meaning of a character is expressed through who he or she is, what he or she does, and how he or she does it; the meaning of a location is most often expressed through the mood it creates; and the meaning of an object is expressed usually through the effect it has on other things or on the characters.

Meaning can take the form of cerebral communication (information presented directly or symbolically) or emotional communication (the imparting of specific emotions). When characters, objects, or locations convey meaning they are significant. Characters, objects, and locations can each be tested by the mechanics' (statics and dynamics) description of forces to be determined as vectors when that description is coupled with the idea of significance. This is an immediate boon to literary and dramatic analysis since it gives a fast, systematic means of sorting through the many objects and places mentioned in stories to determine which are the ones that convey forces. There are novels that list myriad locations and films with casts of thousands, so knowing how to quickly, systematically, and accurately spot the key locales, objects, and characters is extremely useful.

In keeping with the analogy to engineering, significant characters will convey vectors because characters have a variety of ways in which they can move. Their bodies can move; their thoughts can move; and their emotions can move. Characters can create action, atmosphere, and meaning. The meaning characters create can take the form of understanding the character's nature in particular as well as human nature in general. Character has always been considered an essential element (sometimes *the* essential element) of literature and drama.

Objects will be comprised of vectors when the objects can move, when it is their nature to be transported, or when they draw things to or into themselves, and when they convey some sort of meaning. For instance, the painting in *The Picture of Dorian Gray* contains a vector as it draws Dorian's aging unto itself. Also, objects that are meant to be transported frequently convey literary and dramatic vectors. For instance, the purpose of messages is to be transported from one place to another and so messages frequently convy vectors. Innumerable stories, plays, and films hinge on a message being received in some form: letter, telegram, email, phone call, or dream. Gifts, too, are meant to be passed from one person to another, and so will often convey vectors. The nutcracker in *The Nutcracker* ballet is established immediately as a vector carrier because it is a gift; also, it can move (the mouth). Machines and gadgetry can move and so will be a vehicle for vectors, like the pendulum in Edgar Allen Poe's "The Pit and the Pendulum."

When objects meet the quick and dirty rule of moving or drawing things to them and are of significance, then they are analogous to vectors and from here on will be referred to as vector props. In the theater, objects that are used on stage are called "props"; especially those handled by the actors and called "hand props." Props differ from the set dressings (objects set about the stage) in that props are necessary to the script in some way. Props are often vital in establishing character, providing a means for an action to occur, or representing thematic or symbolic elements of the production; therefore the term "prop" already signifies an object with special relevance.

An example of a well known prop is the veil in Nathaniel Hawthorne's "The Minister's Black Veil." A minister known for his mildness becomes a frightening and therefore more effective preacher by always wearing a black veil. A veil is something that is drawn up or drawn down and so moves, thereby meeting the engineers' quick and dirty definition. A black crepe veil has symbolic significance (it is used to indicate mourning), and so meets the criterion of having significance. The veil helps to establish the minister's character, provides the means of the action of the story, and is symbolically necessary to the piece.

By analogy to the engineers' quick and easy means of finding vectors, locations can also convey vectors, since locales can both attract and resist movement. In Chekhov's *The Cherry Orchard* Madame Ranevsky, her family, and the proletariat Lopahin have come to claim possession of the orchard. As the central symbol of the play, the cherry orchard has the power to draw things to it. Similarly, in *King Lear*, England becomes a vector because the character vectors position themselves to obtain it. Cordelia comes from France to confront her sisters about England in England. Thus, England has the power to draw things to it.

A location can also offer resistance. In many a ghost story, a house does not allow the people to open its doors and leave it. A prop can also resist being acted upon. Excalibur could not be removed from the stone by anyone, no matter how he tried, except by Arthur. A character, too, may resist being moved in some way. In Feodor Sologub's "The Uniter of Souls" the character Garmonov manages to resist being united with the other half of his soul, Sonpolyev. A personality trait or an objective which makes a character unyielding is also a form of resistance.

This is the idea inherent in the tragic flaw. The character will have a trait that is immutable, such as Brutus's honor. Regardless of circumstances, the trait remains fixed, showing that the character has a great steadfastness to a particular value or way of being, but the resistance to change eventually brings about the character's doom. Thus, honor becomes one of the vectors of Shakespeare's *Julius Caesar*. A tragic flaw, when discerned, is always attributed to a hero, and the flaw, being a noble quality which nevertheless destroys the hero, is essentially what makes a character particularly significant.

Similarly, an objective that a character is obsessed with is an indicator of a resisting vector. Herman in Alexander Pushkin's "The Queen of Spades" becomes fixated on the idea that following a magical condition when playing three certain cards will win him a fortune. In pursuit of this objective, Hermann frightens an old woman to death, ruins his romance, loses all his money, and goes completely mad.

The antagonist can also have an immutable trait that destroys him. Shylock, in *The Merchant of Venice*, refuses to let go of his desire for revenge—"I will have my bond"—and this results in his losing everything important to him: his money, his goods, and most heartrending of all, his daughter. Here too the refusal to change, the insistence on revenge despite all, is of great significance because it causes so many other events to occur. It puts Antonio in danger of his life. It causes Portia to disguise herself as a man and travel to Venice to act as defense for Antonio. Also, it allows for Lorenzo and Jessica (Shylock's daughter) to marry. A character's having a tragic flaw (refusing to change) or refusing to give up an objective

(Shylock's revenge) is always a matter of significance, and so such a character conveys an important vector.

Finding significance for characters, objects, and locales is done through the already established means of literary and dramatic analysis. For instance, finding the character with a tragic flaw is a traditional literary analytical tool. In theater, the director's question of "who is driving the scene" is a means of determining what character is pivotal to the scene. For Method actors, the most important characters are those whose objectives (an objective is what the character wants) cause the action of the play or film to occur. Likewise, a prop that a character wants badly is significant, such as the title object in Nicolai V. Gogol's story "The Overcoat." A prop that all the characters want is also, significant, such as the gem in Wilkie Collins' *The Moonstone*.

Finding allusions, symbols, and metaphors is an essential of literary analysis and a major form of dramatic analysis. Frequently allusions, symbols, and metaphors take the form of props or locales. The sound of the scythe (an object that is meant to be moved) in Maeterlinck's "The Intruder" is a symbol of death's approach. In *The Cherry Orchard*, the orchard symbolizes the beautiful but no longer fruitful upper classes. The overcoat, with its collar made of cat fur in "The Overcoat," represents the difficulties the poor must endure to acquire creature comforts only to have the hard-won necessities of life stolen from them and the calamity used to abuse them further. The engineering questions of does it move, does it draw or resist things, and is it relevant to the wanted results correspond well with traditional dramatic and literary aesthetic notions of what is deemed a force.

Continuing the analogy to vector theory, once a character, location, or prop has been determined to be conveying vectors, the sense and magnitude can be found. Determining sense matches directly with established literary and dramatic theory. The protagonist and his or her allies are analogous to vectors with positive sense, and the antagonist and his or her cohorts are analogous to vectors with negative sense. Typically, the sense of a location vector will be positive if good things happen to the protagonist there or if it is a good, wholesome, or beautiful place. Shangri-la in *Lost Horizon* is such a case. The sense of a location vector will be negative if bad things happen to the protagonist there or if it is a bad, fouled, ugly, or frightening place such as the Chateau D'If in Dumas's *The Count of Monte Cristo*.

Similarly, in the main, vector props with a positive sense will cause good things to happen, have good effects on the protagonist and/or his or her allies, will be attractive, and/or will allude to good things. For instance, the little bell on the Christmas tree at the close of *It's a Wonderful Life* refers to Clarence the angel getting his wings as well as to heaven and so is a positive prop vector. Most of the time, vector props with a negative sense will cause bad things to happen to the protagonist—but good to the antagonist—and will be ugly, and/or will allude to evil things. In "The Overcoat" Alaky's old coat is a miserable, falling-apart affair representative of the misery of his life and eventually causes his death. Similarly, but in a humorous vein, the debilitating effects of kryptonite on *Superman* are well known, and so kryptonite is a negative prop vector.

Vector theory, however, does not restrict the idea of positive and negative to bad and good. In fact, the idea of sense, of positive and negative, simply indicates that the vectors move in counter ways. So, in more interesting works of literature and drama, the vectors could represent all virtues, but the virtues are different enough from one another to form contrasts. For instance, the values of love and honor are the contrasting vectors in Corneille's *The Cid*. Another example is the vectors of political vision and scientific experience countering the vectors of artistic vision and personal experience in Mikhail Bulgakov's *The Master and Margarita*. Further, a character may convey more than one vector, and so may convey positive and negative sense vectors. This is the case when a character has what is called in dramatic theory "internal conflict." Whichever sense is that of the majority of the character's vectors will be the character's overall way of acting, but the character will at times act in ways reflective of his or her minority sense vectors. *The Strange Case of Dr. Jekyll and Mr. Hyde* is a study of a character split evenly between two sets of vectors, one negative, the other positive. Thus, the idea of sense in vector theory allows for a great range in creation of characters.

The correlations between literary and dramatic analysis and vector theory continue with the concept of magnitude. For characters, locations, and props mere size can be important, and correlates to the idea of line length for magnitude in a mathematical representation of forces. The protagonist and villain are usually tall, especially on stage and screen. The one who is taller is usually the stronger. Vector locations will have great magnitude if they can draw many things to them and draw them swiftly. Size, age, strength, complexity, and unusual powers are all going to be indicators of magnitude. Basically, any adjective that indicates quantity or level of ability describes the magnitude of the vector, whether the vector be in character, location, or prop form.

The notion of direction is also directly analogous to elements within a work of drama or literature. In literature and drama direction can be delineated by two locations that are set up in contrast to each other. If there are, the pathway or course between the two locations demarcates the direction of the locations and character and prop vectors that move between those locales. The novel *The Master and Margarita* has several sets of locales where the direction of forces are established. For instance, Griboyedov House, famous for the prestigious literary club of politically accepted writers who are housed there, and its fancy restaurant, is contrasted with the master's basement apartment which does not have a kitchen. The master's apartment is comfortable; one its of the two rooms is 14 square feet, contrasting with Griboyedov

House, which has an office for housing problems that always has a long queue. Griboyedov House's restaurant is painted with lilac horses; the master's apartment looks out on a garden with lilacs. These contrasts establish the directions of writing accepted/writing banned, feasting/hunger, housing problem/roominess, camaraderie/ostracism, artificiality/ naturalness, supposed artistry/real artistry.

Any contrasts that are stressed are also indications of direction. In Dostoevsky's "The Christmas Tree and the Wedding" the well-dowried girl is contrasted with the poor governess' boy. The well-behaved and presumably educated governess' cherub is contrasted with the boorishness and ugliness of the rich Julian Mastakovich. The lovely girl is not married to the governess' boy to whom she clearly is suited and is fond of—she is married, to her misery, to the rich boor who is two or three times her age. Love/material position, manners/boorishness, innocence/ depravity, greed/want become the directions of the vectors.

As these contrasts show, the directions of the vectors of a dramatic or literary piece are crucial to determine because, taken together, the directions of the various vectors delineate the theme of the work. Students of literature and drama often have great difficulty grasping the concept of theme; therefore, having a ready, systematic means of correctly ascertaining theme is a great benefit. However, the main relevance of the direction is structural. As the forces travel from the onset of the tale to the close, the direction of the vectors may be a direct line from start to climax, change in a zigzag line, or follow the path of a curve depending on how the forces make contact with each other. The graphing of the plot allows for knowing where possible weak points are in the tale's structure as well as showing what type of shape a particular dramatic or literary piece has. While most directors of plays and producers of films do not graph out the structure of the piece on which they are working on paper, they do have a picture of it in their minds and are apt to express it through gesture as they work with the actors. ("It is supposed to build like this, [gesture] but right now it is doing this [gesture]." Or they will makes comments like "It [the scene] is flat"; "Now it [the scene] is building properly."

Besides giving a means of establishing the forces clearly, providing a flexible way of clarifying characterization through magnitude and sense, allowing for an efficient process for ascertaining theme through determining direction, and establishing the overall shape by the demarcation of the forces' directions, the vector theory analogy proffers literary and dramatic analysis a method of examining the workings of rising action, the climax, and the denouement. In dramatic theory, the moment of the onset of the play or film to the moment of climax is referred to as rising action. Rising action consists of exciting moments, when new developments occur, and lulls, moments of quiet activity where the audience is allowed to reflect on what has happened or absorb a particular mood. The denouement, or falling action, begins right after the climax and lasts till the end of the play or film.

Since rising action and falling action are defined in relation to the climax, it is clear that a fundamental requirement of analyzing literature and drama is the ability to spot the climax. Students are told that the climax will be the most exciting moment that comes near the end of the play. Other than this advice, the student must learn to develop an intuition for finding climaxes through dint of practice. What is it that our intuition does when finally it learns to unerringly select the climax? The answer lies in the engineers' notion of the single force that arises when all the forces of a system act together at a common point (Jensen and Chenoweth, 1983, p. 10). This point is directly analogous to literature and drama as the climax. The moment, towards the end of the literary or dramatic work, where all the forces converge at the same place to form one new force is the climactic convergence—the climax—the point in the work that is ultimately transformative. It is this final convergence which involves all of the vectors that gives the work coherence.

During a literary or theatrical piece, the various character, prop, and location vectors are going to converge at different times. They will not all converge at once until the climax, but they will converge in pairs or small clusters. The series of convergences between the various vectors create the rising action of a work of literature and drama. The expression of the resultant of the converging forces forms the lulls, but the transformed forces go on to converge again and again in different groupings until all of the forces converge at the same time and place at the end of the literary or dramatic work. Vector theory allows for a wide variety of plots since what number and combination of convergences and what the number and types of forces at play are is up to the creator of the literary or theatrical piece. Only one convergence is essential—the climax. But if that is the only convergence, the piece will be short.

According to vector theory, the vectors are added or subtracted when they converge. Here again the analogy of vector theory with the workings of plot is highly evocative. If same-sense vectors converge, then they are added together. So, when the protagonist meets his or her allies their magnitudes are united into a new, stronger force. Typically a protagonist becomes much more effective in achieving his or her objective when he or she is united with comrades, and the same goes for the antagonist. Since the characters convey the vectors, the forces can be transferred. For instance, if the protagonist is united with a prop vector, the protagonist can either carry the prop vector about or take what he or she needs from the prop—read the message and then dispose of it.

The protagonist's going to a positive sense location vector will make the protagonist stronger. There is greater safety in being within the castle because the castle adds its magnitude to the protagonist. If the protagonist is relatively weak, and the other positive vector he or she meets is stronger, the protagonist's direction can be shifted. That is, the protagonist will follow an altered direction towards his ultimate objective. Consider the resultant of the meeting graphically. If the protagonist is moving upwards, and he or she meets a strong force moving to the right, the protagonist will still move upwards, but he or she will be shifted to moving to the right as he or she climbs upward. This is in keeping with The Method's notion of the "beat change," or moments when a change of tactic or procedure takes place. A "beat change" is also a moment of a power exchange, which is also in keeping with the idea of what happens when vectors converge. How much magnitude the protagonist gains from the encounter and how big of a change in the protagonist's direction is made increases interest and excitement levels for the reader or audience. Naturally, negative vectors converging—the antagonist with his cohorts, negative vector props, and negative vector locations—will work structurally the same way. Interest value for the reader or audience will occur to the amount of magnitude gained or lost and the degree of change in direction.

According to vector theory, there can also be impacts between the bodies (Jenson and Chenoweth, 1983, p. 414); similarly, between characters there may be actual physical touch. For instance the hero may steal a kiss from the heroine before he dashes off, or the villain may slug the hero and run off. A convergence can result in the destruction of the weaker vector. In literary and dramatic terms, this can range from the destruction of a prop or locale to the killing of a character. Although convergences can be physical—the characters, props, and locations actually coming into contact—the convergence can be of vectors that are ideals or opinions, so vocal exchanges can reflect vectors that are ideas making impact. Interest will be garnered in relation to the magnitude of the vector being destroyed. The stronger the vector is that is destroyed the more interesting or exciting it will be for the reader or audience.

Once a convergence has occurred, there is often a lull. Lulls are the time needed to reveal the transformations of the vectors. Lulls show the altered direction of the force at hand, indicate the magnitude the vector now has, and reveal the sense of the transformed vector. Usually the vectors are still largely intact; i.e., retain their positive or negative sense, and so the different-sense vectors go off on their separate ways. The less time there is between convergences the more quickly paced the work will be.

In dramatic aesthetic theory the rising action is often said to have a "complication." Complications are when the protagonist suffers some sort of reversal. These reversals are readily described by using the vector theory analogy. The protagonist loses some of his or her magnitude in a convergence with the antagonist or other negative vector. This loss of magnitude can take the form of theft or destruction of a vector prop; the protagonist's being caught in a negative vector location; or the protagonist's being physically or mentally restrained or injured. Despite the complication, the protagonist will eventually accumulate enough magnitude through convergences with other positive vectors to overcome the antagonist.

Eventually, the salient forces must converge at the same time and place to form the climax. This can take the form of many characters meeting at the same vector location, or it can take the form of only two vectors, one positive and one negative, coming together at the same time and place. In the case of only two vectors meeting, each vector has accumulated magnitude from previous convergences with same-sense vectors. The more forces present or the greater the magnitude of the forces present at the climactic convergence the more exciting the climax will be for the reader or audience. When the protagonist or the antagonist converge, whichever one has the greatest magnitude becomes triumphant. The level of triumph is equal to the amount of force still extant after the convergence. If the opposing forces are nearly matched the triumph will be modest; if the opposing forces are widely disparate in magnitude, then the triumph of the stronger force will be great. It is also possible that the forces will produce a direct impact and destroy the main characters, the place of convergence, and any significant prop.

Not all works have all the forces tidily converging at the same time and place; however, there will be one convergence that has most of the forces converging. Those few forces that do not converge at the climax will converge right after it, forming part of the falling action. It is necessary for all the forces to finally converge, either together at the climax or with a small number of forces converging right after the climax for the structure to be complete.

The falling action, the denouement, of the literary or dramatic piece is the resultant of the climactic convergence. The falling action, then, reveals the sense, magnitude, and direction of the transformed force. Thus, even when the protagonist is triumphant, he or she is not who he or she was at the onset of the literary or dramatic piece. This idea of transformation is very important to literary and dramatic aesthetics, for it is an important means of imparting instruction or values and gives much of the satisfaction audiences and readers are looking for. For this reason, if the denouement is missing the work will seem pointless, unfinished, and unsatisfying. Readers and audiences wish to have a general idea of what is left of the forces of the piece and where those forces are going in order to feel satisfied. The denouement shows exactly what the transformation is. The new direction shows which way in life the character will follow; the new sense lets the reader or audience know if it is the protagonist or antagonist who has triumphed; the new magnitude reveals how much strength the character now has. Any forces that did not converge during the climax will converge during the denouement and will have resultants in keeping with the resultant with the climax. For example, if the protagonist was triumphant at the climax, any lesser characters who had positive sense will meet with success in some way.

Further, the audience or reader, to be satisfied, needs to feel that the work is finished rather than that it has merely stopped. Therefore, since most works consist of more than one convergence, the audience or reader usually needs some indication that no further convergences will be forthcoming. This is usually accomplished by the distancing of the reader or audience from the resulting vectors. If a distance or separation is not made, the reader or audience will want and expect more. Easing the reader or audience from the literary or dramatic work is known in literary theory as closure.

When nothing is left from the impact, either the audience is purged of the emotions the work created in them, allowing for a catharsis, or the forces will return to the order they were in at the beginning of the piece when presumably they were in balance. In either case, the audience or reader is satisfyingly disengaged from the literary or dramatic work. In the case of the climactic convergence having a resultant, the newly transformed force is completely unencumbered. There are no forces to converge with it to alter or to stop it in any way and so the force moves along its direction away from the reader or audience. Thus, in the cowboy movies, the hero rides off into the sunset; in the fairy tales, "everybody lives happily ever after"; and in the theater there is a silence as the lights dim and go out. The denouement, then, is the segment of the literary or dramatic work that finishes the work by manifesting the transformation of the climactic convergence's resultant and by providing closure.

Vectorial analysis illuminates the components of creative writings; delineates the rising action; facilitates the accurate pinpointing of climaxes; reveals why the falling action is necessary and what the falling action consists of; and ties together old and new aesthetic concepts, such as the tragic flaw, beat changes, and catharsis. The theory of vectors as an analytical tool fulfills the needs of dramatic and literary theory.

Chapter Three
Vector Qualities:
Sense, Direction, and Magnitude

In vectorial analysis, vectors are said to have the three qualities of sense, direction, and magnitude. *Magnitude* refers to the idea that forces are quantifiable in some way. *Direction* is the course-way along which the vector moves, the trajectory of the force's line of action. *Sense* is how the force moves: up, right, clockwise all being positive; down, left, and counterclockwise being negative.

SENSE

Since vectorial sense is either positive or negative, the simplest way of apprising the sense of a vector is determining how a character, prop, or locale is described. The adjectives and adverbs used to describe characters, locales, and props often reveal the sense. Those characters, plots, and locales that are characterized as negative or bad have negative sense while those characters, plots, and locales that are characterized as positive or good have positive sense. This means of determining sense is usually sufficient for works that are meant as light entertainment. For more sophisticated literary and dramatic works using the concept of sense is also useful.

More sophisticated works rarely tell the reader or audience directly what a character's sense is; they ask the reader to discover it. So, another means of determining the sense of a vector is to ascertain whether an element in a tale is allied with or opposed to a value the author considers good. What values the author champions will indicate the sense of the positive vectors. The protagonist will support the values held by the author; the antagonist will oppose them. The terms *protagonist* and *antagonist* mean exactly that—one who is for is the protagonist; one who is against is the antagonist. Determining the values the author deems good may sound nebulous, but can be quite easily discerned when a work is analyzed through one of the most important forms of study contributed by modern dramatic aesthetics: Stanislavsky's system of analyzing plays, known in the United States as The Method.

The sense of an element in a work of fiction is the judgment value that can be determined for the objective of a character. What is it that the character wants? In answering this quintessential question of The Method, not only does the actor find the key to his or her role, but the values of the author stand revealed. Hamlet wants to avenge his father's death; Batman wants to save Gotham City; Everyman wants to go to Heaven; Marian Halcombe in Wilkie Collins' *The Woman in White* wants to rescue her sister from the machinations of Count Fosco and Sir Percival. Each of these are motivations that the authors clearly found laudable. Thus, Hamlet, Batman, Everyman, and Marian Halcombe all have positive senses. Objectives of favorite villains, on the other hand, clearly show what the authors found detestable: Lady Macbeth wants to usurp the crown; the fisherman in Seami's "Hagoromo" wants to steal the angel's wings; Medea wants to avenge herself on her husband. Each of these objectives is presented as nefarious. Thus, the senses of forces in plays and stories and the sense's alignment with the author or playwright's values are usually expressed by the virtue or wickedness of the characters' objectives.

Sense can additionally be analyzed in the way engineers define sense. Sense in engineering is defined as how a force behaves. This relates directly to literature and drama in that how a character behaves can be analyzed as how the forces the character embodies behave. Is the force moving up or down, right or left, clockwise or counter-clockwise? These different ways of behaving have cultural associations. It will be readily apparent to most that the delegating of up, right, and clockwise to the positive and down, left, and counterclockwise to the negative is because of Western cultural associations. Up is towards heaven, so naturally up is going to be positive while down, towards hell, is negative. Similarly, right is the way of the righteous, and so must be positive, and left being the "left-handed way" or sinister must be negative. Hurricanes, tornadoes, and draining, circling water in the western hemisphere move in a clockwise manner; therefore anything moving counterclockwise will be unnatural, and of course what is unnatural is frightening and bad and so negative. Vector theory already has as a base culturally defined associations.

This means that sense can be analyzed in literature and drama in the same way that engineers define sense. Again, sense in engineering is defined as how a force behaves. This relates directly to literature and drama in that characters' characteristic behavior is caused by the characteristic behavior of the forces that affect the character. For instance, a character's behavior can be summed up by such phrases as "leftist," "fools around," "on the up-and-up," "dregs of the universe," etc. Each of these phrases relates to orientation of movement just as sense does in vector theory. Even "dregs of the universe" relates to the orientation of movement in that dregs are at the bottom and so refer to what is moving downwards. Different ways of behavior are commonly described as directional (Standard English meaning)—left or right, up or down, forwards or backwards, clockwise or counterclockwise, or cardinally (north or south, east or west) in these culturally determined sorts of phrases.

The table here gives examples of the different cultural associations given to ways of behaving.

Behavior	View	Associations
Up	Christian	Heavenly, angelical, honest ("upright," "on the up-and-up")
	Colloquial	PuritanWork-Ethic, dreamy ("head in the clouds"), inattentive ("Es-tu a la lune?"), drugged ("spaced out"), crazy ("mind is gone"), Uncertain ("things are up in the air"). Original/creative/excellent ("far out"), happy ("upbeat")
Down	Christian	Hellish, evil, sinful, sexual.
	Modern Psychological	Depressed, poor or homeless ("down on his luck").
Left	Christian	Sinister, evil, untruthful, deviant.
	Political	Communist ("leftist").

Right	Christian	Righteous, correct, honest, truthful, moral ("right on my side"), ethical.
	Colloquial	Stodgy, conservative ("square").
	Political	Reactionary, excessively conservative.
Clockwise	Political/ American	Mainstream, focus on ("circle in on"), surround, corral, affect others gently but surely ("ripple out"), engagement/marriage (putting on of ring).
Counter-clockwise	Political/ American	Against the mainstream, being lost ("going round in circles"), aimless activity, wasting time ("twiddling your thumbs"), causing trouble ("making waves"), romantic breach or divorce (taking off of ring).

In addition to these behaviors that are commonly considered by engineers, literature adds:

Behavior	View	Associations
Forward	American	Progressive, visionary ("forward thinker"), avant garde, honest ("straightforward")
Backward	American	uncivilized, retarded, excessively conservative, lacking in skills or ability ("Lagging behind"), hindrance ("setback").

North	American	Guiding light ("North star"), Abolitionist.
	North European	Deadly cold, darkness (from associations with winter), evil spirits (from Norse Evil Ice Giants, etc.)
South	American	Left-handed ("south-paw"), hot, steamy, sexual, gentility ("Southern Hospitality")
West	American	Gold, opportunity, lawlessness ("the Wild West")
	North American and European	"First world" (as opposed to "third world"), end of the day's labor, end of life, the finish, (from the Irish Celt) land of summer and flowers where heroes go (the "Western Paradise")
	Buddhist	Paradise (the "Western Paradise")
East	American	Education (from Ivy league and other universities located in Eastern US), culture, idealism, chilly and reasonable fear of the former Soviet Regime, mysterious, exotic (as in Far Eastern cultures), New beginnings, new chances, fresh starts in life ("dawn of a new day"), dueling, (traditionally met at dawn), hard worker (gets up at the "crack of dawn").

From this chart it is clear that the context of the literary or dramatic piece is crucial to determining the sense of forces. In one context, a hot, steamy, tropical island can be a sexual paradise (positive sense); and in another context the same island and its goings-on can be a "den of iniquity" (negative sense). Further, the cultural contexts can indicate how different forces affect a character, prop, or locale. For instance, American spy films, prior to the fall of the Wall of Berlin, loved to have Russian women as characters. On the one hand the Russian woman represented the negative forces connoted by American associations with the Soviet Union, and on the other hand, the Russian woman represented the forces of mystery and exotica connoted by American associations with the East. Looking for cultural associations and metaphorically implicit language is part of the work of metaphorical analysis. Utilizing vector theory's notion of sense as types of behavior assists in metaphorical analysis's character analysis.

For instance, the main character Joan Froser in *Children of the Revolution* is affected by three forces: one force moving left—of the political left, or communist; another force moving up—angelically; and another force moving counterclockwise—going in circles backwards. Joan Froser is a communist, what is also called an extreme leftist. When asked to marry someone—offered a wedding ring—she runs off to Russia and makes love to a Soviet spy and Lenin in the same evening which is behavior that is the reverse of pursuing the normal course of a ring. The symbol of marriage is a ring, so the positive force of marriage would be moving clockwise. Instead of accepting marriage, Joan "fools around"—behaves as a force going counterclockwise. Joan bears Lenin's child, and brings the boy up in a good, loving home, filling his head with the high ideals of working for the betterment of hard-working people. Joan's loving bringing up of her son and her dedication to the ideals of improving working people's lives are all very positive qualities, and so on the up/down (heaven/hell) course way she is clearly positive. The three forces of leftist politics (negative sense), running around from man to man in her love-life (negative sense), and maintaining an uplifting, idealist love for her child and her fellows (positive sense) make Joan a complicated, comical, endearing, but ultimately tragic character.

This example shows how finding the words and phrases of motion—up or down, left or right, and circling clockwise or counterclockwise— associated with the behavior of a character readily indicate the sense and help to distinguish the differing forces at play in literary or dramatic construction. How a character behaves relates to how a force behaves (moves) and in that way indicates the sense of the character vector.

Since characters, props, and settings can embody one or more forces, the quality of sense yields a variety of uses for plot construction. Characters, props, and settings can maintain one sense strongly and steadfastly throughout the work. Plays of the neoclassical ideal— namely the works of Moliere, Racine, and Corneille—follow this use of sense. The heroes are always brave and honest; the ingénues are strictly sweet and innocent; the villains consistently villainous; the wise never lose their good judgment. The neoclassical aesthetic concept of verisimilitude held that things are absolute and so characters were expected to be what we would now call "one sided." The characters embodied one force and so had one sense, and that was it. Most other forms of literature and drama find the neoclassical notion of verisimilitude unbelievable, wanting characters of more depth and complexity. As in the film *Children of the Revolution*, countering forces working within one character enables authors to create characterizations of dimension.

Additionally, vector theory's concept of sense is very useful in understanding how and why character behavior is influenced. In dramatic and literary aesthetics, it is understood that the characters, props, and locales can and do influence each other. Indeed, the influencing of a character by another has often been the subject of literary and dramatic works. In vectorial terms, characters, props, and settings can be affected by countering forces so that the character, prop, or setting seems to change their nature depending on who or what is around them.

The film *Father Flanagan's Boys Town* is about how a character can affect the character of other characters. One character can bring out another's better nature, as in *Boys Town*. The film *Twins* works with this device of sense, too. One twin is short, unfit, unattractive, and inclined to immoral behavior. The other twin is tall, muscle bound, muscle bound, and wholly moral in behavior. When the twins unite the immorally inclined one becomes more and more honest through his association with his brother. The mannerisms of the twins are shown to be the same, making the unattractive twin appealing. Similarly, in both versions of the film *We're No Angels*, convicts escape and hide out among very good people. Since they cannot let the good people know they are criminals, the convicts try to behave as well as the people they find themselves among. The degree to which they fail in this is comical; the degree to which they succeed is touching. Through being among good people the convicts become better people themselves. The positive sense of the many vectors around them nullify the convicts' negative sense (to a great extent) and strengthens the convicts' positive sense.

Props, too, can behave differently depending on where they are put or who is handling them. For instance, it is well known that kryptonite has a debilitating effect on Superman while it harms no-one else. Kryptonite and Superman are affected by forces normal humans are not, and the non-earthly force emanating from kryptonite is a countering force to the non-earthly force moving Superman. Settings are the least changeable in sense, but they too can be influenced by characters or things. In the story of the Buddha, for instance, flowers are said to have sprouted from the ground where the infant Siddhartha walked.

What is happening in these cases is that one of the two bodies (character, prop, or setting) is propelled by both positive and negative vectors. The forces of the other body are mostly or completely one sense, and so the adding together of the similar sense forces of the two bodies (any combination of characters, props, or locale vectors with each other) overpowers any effects the opposite sense force may have. Therefore the convicts in *We're No Angels*, the bad twin in *Twins,* and the delinquents in *Boys Town*, all behave better among the positive forces of the good people around them because their own negative forces are negated and their positive forces reinforced. Thus, a character, prop, or setting can act very differently depending on who or what is around it.

Another case of a character being affected by more than one force is the contemporary dramatic aesthetic notion of "internal conflict." Being torn by the forces within one's self to behave in countering ways is an experience which many modern audiences relate to, and so audiences find works of fiction and drama more realistic when characters grapple with this problem. Ibsen's *Ghosts* is realistic to contemporary audiences, unlike the first audiences who saw it, because the character of the mother is trapped in internal conflict. Should she give her son poison as he requested when he becomes insane from venereal disease, or not? To give it is his request and arguably merciful, but doing so would make her her son's killer.

Characters, props, and locales can also seem to be one sense, but actually have another. The sense is consistent, but new information brings to light its true nature. An example of mistaken sense is in the film, *Babette's Feast.* Babette is characterized by evil witch imagery. She arrives on stormy seas wearing a black cape and carrying a cage of small, agitated birds. The townspeople express fear over the meal she is to serve. Nevertheless, by the end of the film she is revealed as a wonderful culinary wizard. The scary looking birds she carries are delicacies for the meal she prepares with the money she won from a lottery. The stormy seas can be taken as a symbol of life's troubles and how they can be survived by the magic of the complete generosity she shows when she uses her winnings to prepare and serve to others a fine evening meal. The frightening witch's cape is both an invisibility cloak and curse; it has hidden Babette's true identity in a way detrimental to Babette herself. Babette makes the lives of the townspeople better, and she does it through the magical art of her cooking even while they do not see who she really is. Once the character force (or prop or locale) has enough magnitude it can reveal its true sense, and this happens to Babette through the winning of the lottery.

When characters have more than one force affecting their behavior, readers and audiences feel that the characters have dimension. Dimension is yet another concept that is directly analogous with vector theory. Just as in aesthetics, dimension in vector theory refers to how many qualitative elements there may be. The more forces a character, prop, or setting is affected by, the more dimension it has. Therefore an accounting of the different ways the quality of sense is evident in a character, prop, or locale is useful in analyzing dimension. Traditional analysis of stories and plays have encompassed determining character type through the work's descriptors of the character; placing value judgments on characters' actions; examining characters' internal conflict (if any), establishing metaphorical associations with characters' behavior; and seeking signs of dimension in characters. All of these are supported, facilitated, broadened, and unified by vector theory's notion of sense.

By regarding characters, props, and locales as bodies that can be affected by any number of forces, vector theory unites such disparate ideas as neoclassical verisimilitude with the modern concept of internal conflict. In the case of verisimilitude there is one force with one sense in one character; in the case of internal conflict there are different forces with different senses in the protagonist or other major character. Character type and character behavior are explicitly related by vector theory by defining sense as how forces behave. The influence of one character on another (or any combination of character/prop/locale influences) is also described readily and in detail by vector theory. Sense defines why character can be consistent and why character can be altered and how much under what conditions. Defining seemingly disparate behavior— moving to the right and moving in circles clockwise—as being of the same sense broadens the range of activities in which a character can engage and still be considered consistent with a character's type; while disparate behavior such as lofty movement (Dr. Jekyll's high-minded experiments) and sinister movement (Mr. Hyde's activities) can be found to be realistic to readers and audiences when convergence with another vector (as represented by the potion) is shown to have caused the separation of good and bad forces within a particular body. Knowing what to look for—descriptors, the ways of behaving indicated by culturally defined metaphoric statements of orientations of movement, the number of ways of behaving a character, prop, or locale—shows auctorial value judgments on behavior; and knowing why to look for these things, makes analysis easier and faster.

DIRECTION

Movement, flow, rhythm, pacing: these are terms typical in dramatic aesthetics. Establishing proper movement, flow, rhythm, and pacing are basic to every production's rehearsal process. Yet, like the term climax, these terms are not precisely defined and are only intuitively understood after a great deal of onerous skill development. Looking at the terms it is clear that they imply that something, probably a character, is going from one place to another. This is the case, but the "places" are not ultimately locations; they are achievements or changes of states of being.

The term *flow* is about the production's conveying the feeling that all the elements of the production harmoniously move together along a course way. The term *rhythm* is about shaping the flow—sometimes fast, sometimes slow; sometimes loud, and sometimes soft—so that the movement is engaging to the audience. *Pacing* is about setting speeds for the physical movement such as "crosses" (the actor's movement across the stage space) and delivery of lines—how lines are said quickly or slowly, etc. When a director says "Pick up the pace," he or she means the actors should deliver lines more quickly, pick up on cues (allow for no pauses between when one person speaks and another replies), and execute blocking (the traffic, the crosses from one part of the stage to another) or any and all actions more quickly. Pacing also has to do with how well interest levels are kept. Speed does not always equate to interest, so some moments must have a slower pace or sometimes a hiatus of action to keep or heighten interest.

Movement is a crucial concept to dramatic aesthetics. The movement of a theatrical piece has to do with how frequently events occur, how long the events take to happen, and how smoothly or unevenly the events are related to each other. The term *movement*, then, encompasses pacing, flow, and rhythm. Movement is about the pacing, flow, and rhythm being dynamically combined into one organic whole or, as the mathematicians say, one system. The movement is seen to be purposeful in that it seems to get somewhere. This is where the difference between storyline and plot is important. Storyline is a narrative; plot is a sequence of events that are specifically, rhythmically paced and ordered so that they cause the characters (most often), props, and locales to move from one state to another state in a way that the reader or audience will find meaningful, interesting, and emotionally satisfying. Plot is, therefore, a dramatic structure in the sense that the purpose of plot is to compel the reader or audience's attention through the engagement of the reader or audience's emotions to create a transformation of emotion or state of being.

Storyline, as a narrative, need be no more exciting than a psychologist's case history report. A narrative only becomes dramatic when it is shaped, given a structured build of excitement that results in a transformation. When a narrative succeeds in attaining a dramatic build, its elements become more than individuals, things, and places; the elements become vectors driving the characters, props, and locales. Because the character vectors, prop vectors, or even locale vectors are specifically ordered in drama and literature, a plot can actually be plotted (diagramed), and every "successful" dramatic piece has the same basic shape: a line that for most of its length rises or follows a curve upwards, peaks or attains an apogee, and then what is left of its remainder slopes or follows a curve downward.

For dramatic and literary works, this means that the characters, props, and locales must seem to follow a course. They must have started somewhere to go somewhere. This is standard dramatic aesthetic theory; indeed, it is the basis of metaphorical analysis. The depiction of this course is a major concern in determining the production image. Rarely is this course a road between two places. In some cases it is, like the Yellow Brick Road in the Hollywood film *The Wizard of Oz*, but even in this film the Yellow Brick Road is a symbol for the path which extends from being lost to being enlightened.

Further, the course need not be created by cause and effect. The course may be completely episodic in nature. *The Odyssey,* perhaps the most famous of episodic works, is full of adventures that do not rely on cause or effect. One such adventure is when Odysseus passes the island of the Sirens. Odysseus' ship was lost at sea, and while he was trying to return home to Greece, he just happened to pass the island of the Sirens. Odysseus had himself bound to the masts and his crew plugged their ears. That way the crew would hear neither the Sirens' songs nor Odysseus' commands and so would not be lured nor ordered too near the rocks. However, the bound Odysseus could hear the Siren's songs. Nothing in particular caused the passing by the isle of the Sirens; nothing resulted from Odysseus listening to the Sirens. Nevertheless, that passage in the epic is one of the more memorable scenes. It speaks of the universal understanding that at times we wish to listen to communications that are too sublime to be ordinarily heard; that Odysseus can and does find a way to listen to the Sirens, and tells us that yes, sometimes, the sublime will be in our reach if we properly prepare ourselves for it. As a scene about the resolution of inner yearnings, the story about the Sirens allows for one emotional understanding (acknowledgement of a dangerous desire, a need for the sublime) to lead to another emotional understanding (dangerous desires can be satisfied if precautions are taken; the sublime must be approached with complete surrender and stillness). Like the *Odyssey,* many works of literature and theater are episodic, as Aristotle pointed out, and follow a course of events that extend from one emotional understanding to a very different emotional understanding.

Episodic works rely on direction not just for the shape of plot, but also for cohesion. Normally there is one general direction that creates the basic plot: Odysseus is attempting to go home after the war in Troy; Vladimir and Estragon are awaiting Godot; Don Quixote is following the life of the chivalrous knight errant. Within the basic line of action of the central character's force, many other forces with different directions come into play. Yet, no matter how many other forces come to affect the main character or characters, the other forces always end up driving the main character vector along the pre-established direction. Odysseus must run from the Cyclops towards home;

Vladimir and Estragon must come back again the next day in order to keep waiting for Godot; Don Quixote must keep seeking dragons to slay and damsels to save be they only windmills and tormentors.

The direction of the main vector creates what is known in dramatic aesthetics to actors as a through-line: a line of meaning that is being followed regardless of what else occurs. The through-line, the direction of the primary vector, serves to relate the different vectors of episodic works, thereby giving episodic pieces needed cohesion. In The Method, the objective provides the through-line: e.g. Odysseus wants to go home; Vladimir and Estragon want Godot, Don Quixote wants to slay dragons and rescue damsels. The character objectives of The Method demonstrate how related direction and sense are. The objective is or provides the actor with the through-line, which is the direction, the course way. The judgment value that is made about that objective is the sense of vector, whether it is a negative or positive vector. Through-lines are felt in The Method to be needed for all roles whether in episodic or cause and effect works.

Between the two types of basic plot structures, episodic and cause and effect, there is a huge array of events which can occur in theatrical and literary works. The most obvious are the arguments, fights, love scenes, and buffoonery. Less obvious events, but often more important, are moments when characters come to some kind of realization and change what they do or who they are as a result of it. Whatever type the events are, and most theatrical works make use of a variety of events, they must all eventually follow the same course for the production to have a satisfying sense of movement. Not all the events need to begin on the same course, but they must all end up following the same course. The Cowardly Lion, the Tin Man, and the Scarecrow have different objectives than does Dorothy, but they join with her to follow the same course, the Yellow Brick Road, to reach the same destination—the Wizard of Oz and self-realization. The Cowardly Lion, the Tin Man, the Scarecrow, and Dorothy are easily recognized as different vectors with the same sense (positive) that also have the same direction (the Yellow Brick Road).

Literary and dramatic pieces for sophisticated readers and audiences often make use of subplots and storylines that are separate from the main story, but follow it thematically, often intertwining with the main storyline. This, just as in the *Wizard of Oz* example, is the case of different vectors paralleling or even sharing the same direction as the primary vector moves along, until the other vectors converge with the primary vector. For instance, in *King Lear,* the stories of Edmund and Edgar are subplots. The story of Edgar parallels the story of Cordelia; a virtuous child (Cordelia, Edgar) being cast out in favor of a scheming, wicked child (Edmund, Goneril and Regan). The story of Edmund is more complicated and intertwines with the stories of Goneril and Regan. Eventually the subplots of the stories of Edmund and Edgar are united with the main storyline. Edmund, while dying, reveals the treachery of Goneril and Regan and tries to take back the death warrant he had signed for Lear and Cordelia. Edgar is recognized as the one to reign after Lear. In some films, two entirely different story-lines eventually are merged into one. This is known as parallel editing. The most famous example of parallel editing is in D. W. Griffith's *Birth of a Nation* (1915). In both cases--the use of subplots and the use of parallel editing—the story lines all merge to follow one course. The vectors are shown to have or come to have the same direction.

Each force within a literary and dramatic work will have a direction. Therefore if the characters, props, and locales all embody more than one vector there can be a huge array of directions (course-ways), but all of the directions must ultimately be united into the same direction. Just as sense can be kept hidden as a dramatic device, so can direction. Mysteries and thrillers derive their suspense from the question of direction: what is the path the vector, as it affects a character, is following? An example where direction is kept hidden in order to create suspense is Wilkie Collins' *The Woman in White*. It is quite clear that Marian Halcombe, her sister Lady Laura, and Mr. Hartright are positive vectors; that is, they are representations of positive vectors. Their directions are also known: Lady Laura is on the course of marriage, with the negative sense of her direction being her ill-fated marriage to Sir Percival and the positive sense her final marriage to Mr. Hartright. Marian follows the path of devoted sister, with the negative sense of following her into danger and the positive sense of rescuing her sister from danger. Mr. Hartright follows the course of lover, with the negative sense of being rejected for being poor and the positive sense of being accepted for being true-hearted. Mr. Fairlie (Marian and Laura's uncle), Sir Percival, Count Fosco, and Countess Fosco are all known to be negative vectors. However, the directions of Sir Percival and the Count and Countess are mysterious. The Count's direction is particularly mysterious because, although he is a cohort of Sir Percival and therefore a negative vector, the Count often behaves in a positive manner. For instance, Laura reports, "...he was all kindness and attention...he several times checked Sir Percival's outbreaks of temper, and in the most considerate manner towards me. Perhaps I dislike him because he has so much more power over my husband than I have...All I know is, that I do dislike him" (Collins, p. 232). The taking of Lady Laura's family fortune is not really what the Count is about, although stealing her fortune is definitely what he does try to do. The mystery of the Count's direction is what gives so much of the book its suspense.

In tragedies, the direction is that of life and death with all the vectors eventually converging to create a negative vector of death or ruination. The sense of tragedy is created by the utter relentlessness with which all the vectors speedily and unalterably fall into the same sense—

negative—regardless of how positive each vector may have been at the beginning. John Sinhge's one-act masterpiece *Riders to the Sea* is a typical example of this. The father of the family has long ago died at sea while trying to earn a living by fishing. The main body of play is devoted to how the eldest son who was also fishing to support the family has also just died at sea. The mother implores the youngest son not to go out to sea, for he too will die if he does. Nevertheless, he goes out to sea to fish and provide a living for the family, and dies. The sea is the source of the family's livelihood, but it is also the cause of its ruination. It is clear from the first word of the play that this family is doomed.

King Lear in contrast to *Riders to the Sea* has a vast number of vectors. Nevertheless, just like *Riders to the Sea* the directions of the vectors are relentlessly oriented along the negative sense; everyone is doomed to suffer, and all but one protagonist is doomed to die. The direction of familial love (in the forms of Lear and his daughters and Gloucester and his sons) goes the negative way of blindness to the truth (and literal blindness in the case of Gloucester) and heart break (literally in the case of Lear's death). The direction of change of power, instead of taking the positive sense Lear had intended of domestic fairness, takes the negative sense of civil war. In tragedy, regardless of what the main character may do to alter his or her sense, and regardless of what other vectors come into play, all the vectors become relentlessly negative. It is clear that the directions of the vectors, the course-ways, could lead to success and joy, but the power and horror of tragedies is that regardless, every vector is revealed as a negative force, following the trajectory to doom instead of fortune.

For example Sophocles' *Oedipus Rex* opens with the city in trouble. No matter what Oedipus does to solve the crisis, no matter who comes to help, everyone and everything is irrevocably drawn down the road to disaster. Advice from the Oracle of Delphi has been sought, and only sends back a terrible message; Oedipus's parents are questioned and found not to be his true parents; the Queen is enlisted for compassion, but quickly it is seen she is part of the problem. The oracle, the peasant parents, the Queen, all turn out to have been part of Oedipus's beginnings, but not in the benign way he hopes, and all are also a part of his end. The directions are: fate, with *kismet,* or purposeless fate the negative sense, and fortune or purposeful fate the positive sense; parentage, with biological as the negative sense and adoptive as the positive; kingship, with corruption the negative sense (as the king is the city, how he fares is how the city fares) and stewardship on the positive; and queenship or generativeness, with bearing an heir being the negative vector and generating accord the positive. (The townspeople call on her to settle disputes between her brother and her husband.). One of the ironies in *Oedipus Rex* that is typical of tragedies is that things that ought to be of positive sense, such as bearing an heir, are given a negative sense. The thematic importance of the directions of the vectors (fate, life and death, parentage, etc.) and their convergences yielding negative resultants shape the plot of tragedies and give tragedies their highly emotive value.

In comedies, direction is used to create humor by juxtaposing unrelated vectors with each other. Often the vectors are not allowed to converge and it is the missing of the convergence ("near miss") that is funny; this is the structure of much farce. Another use of direction for comedic effect is when two vectors are expected to converge in one way but do so in another.

In the film *Topper Returns* (Reisz and Millar, pp. 105-107) a funny scene is created out of both techniques. In the scene, a character named Eddie approaches a chair—Eddie represents one vector, the chair another—and when he sits down in it, instead of being comfortably seated, he is tossed down into a well. In this case, the resultant of the convergence was not what was expected. During Eddie's disaster with the chair, Mr. and Mrs. Topper are having an argument and do not see what happens to Eddie although it occurs right under their noses. In this case, the Eddie and chair vectors do not converge with the Topper vectors; the juxtaposition of the unrelated vectors is comical as is their unexpected failure to converge. Then Mr. Topper sits in the chair, and he does *not* fall down the well. Since a negative resultant was expected—his being thrown into the well—but does not occur, humor is created. Eddie warns about the chair's treachery and demonstrates it, falling again into the well, but the resultant, the reaction of the Toppers, is again unexpected: "What a silly way to leave a room."

While the unexpectedness of the resultants is a key element of the humor, the unrelatedness of the vectors' directions is also essential. A man, a chair, and a well, are not normally set together, and they are definitely not normally set beside a couple having a marital argument. The suspense about whether the Toppers will notice the man falling down the well is used for comedic effect when the Toppers don't notice, but the man is not hurt. Anticipation also adds to the humor of the scene, in that the audience expects Mr. Topper to also be pitched into the well, but the anticipated event does not occur to the audience's amusement.

In theatrical aesthetics, it is a basic that some plots derive and build excitement from anticipation and some from suspense. Anticipation is at work in pieces where the audience or reader knows what will happen but not how. Greek audiences, for example, knew the stories behind their plays before they saw the tragedies and comedies, but how the playwright would handle the stories was not known. Thus, the audience knew that Oedipus had killed his father and married his mother, but they did not know how Oedipus was to find he had done this. Tragedies tend to be built on anticipation in that the audience does know what is going to happen—the characters are going to suffer more and more.

In mysteries and melodramas readers or audiences do not know what is going to happen next. Unlike melodramas (mysteries are actually a type of melodrama) which emphasize suspense, and tragedies which emphasize anticipation, thrillers often make an interplay of the two; sometimes the events are expected—anticipated—by the reader or audience, and at other times the reader or audience does not know—they are kept in suspense. Two common techniques in thrillers are: one, for the audience or reader to be expecting a character vector to converge with a negative vector only to be surprised by a convergence with a positive vector; and, two, to have the audience or reader experience a false sense of security where a character vector is expected to be safe but is surprised by a convergence with a negative vector. The course-way of the main vector, the direction of the protagonist is, in thrillers, altered by unexpected vectors which converge with the protagonist. However, just as unexpected, the protagonist out-maneuvers the other vectors to maintain his or her own sense and direction and force them to be destroyed.

Comedies, too, bounce back and forth between anticipation and suspense in order to constantly create unexpected convergences by using the unrelated directions of the vectors. Thus, anticipation and suspense can be created through manipulation of direction. If the direction is unknown, then the reader or audience will not know what to expect next because they will not know where things are going. The reader or audience will be in suspense. If however, the reader or audience knows precisely what is going to occur—that is, they know what the course of events will be, what the direction is, but they do not know how the events will form—then they are in a state of anticipation.

Incidentally, while melodramas as a class of drama have a bad reputation, there are some that are masterpieces. *Cyrano De Bergerac* comes to mind immediately. The reason why the very term melodrama has a negative connotation is that so many melodramas are written by formula. When a play relies on suspense—an audience's not knowing what will happen next—and the play follows a readily recognizable formula, the suspense is destroyed and the quality that was to make the work exciting is missing.

The mathematical concept of direction as the course along which forces travel concurs with theatrical aesthetic notions of movement and the line movement forms as the shape, structure, build, or plot of a literary or dramatic work. The notion of direction fits well with the Aristotlean understanding of episodic and cause and effect types of works, and it also fits with the modern ideas of through-line and characters' objectives. The notion of direction also sheds light on the structural differences between comedies, mysteries, and tragedies while at the same time showing the same principle is at work: forces move along course-ways. As has been stated in the previous chapter, the concept of direction also serves to delineate theme through giving a systematic and definite means of analysis for determining beginning and end points. Understanding the process underlying the categorizations of plot types leads to greater understanding of theatrical and literary pieces and greater facility in creating them.

MAGNITUDE

Magnitude is the third quality vector theory attributes to forces. Magnitude is basically any quantifiable measurement. As such, it shows how much power a force has. Power for characters can come in the form of size, strength, health, beauty, intellect, wisdom, talent, skill, or personality (charismatic, magnetic, stubborn, even repulsive). Power for props can come in the form of size, strength, durability, ability, beauty, draw, and repulsiveness. Power for locales can come in the form of size, intensity and variety of atmosphere, things it can do, beauty, draw, and repulsiveness. Magnitude gives the force its power to move along its direction and to reveal its sense. When the magnitude is low, the force is not very effective and cannot repel other forces well; it cannot draw other things to it successfully; it cannot propel things much; and because of these reasons its sense will be hard to distinguish.

Frequently dramatic and literary pieces begin with the protagonist having a fairly low magnitude. Through meetings with other same sense vectors in the form of other characters, props, and locales, the protagonist builds up his magnitude until he or she is able to defeat the antagonist. This is one of the most simple and basic devices for the use of magnitude in dramas with a happy ending and comedies. In dramas that end unhappily and in tragedies, the protagonist often begins with a great deal of magnitude but loses it through the course of the work to the antagonist who becomes more powerful. In the short story "To Build a Fire" a human protagonist is set against the forces of the Artic. As a Man pitted against Nature who assumes he can master it, the protagonist learns how his efforts are actually feeble against the intense cold, snow, isolation, and dark of the arctic winter.

Characters, props, and locales can give their magnitude to each other since what is occurring is that their vectors are being added to a recipient body. This is why information, money, or gifts passed from one character to another or found in or taken from a locale by a character makes the recipient more powerful. The recipient has added the magnitude of another vector to its own vectors and so has become more powerful. If gifts, information, money, etc. are stolen from the character or locale, then the character or locale vector has subtracted the power that was of the vector of the stolen item.

Like sense, magnitude can also be hidden in that the vector that really has the greatest magnitude is disguised by the body that it is affecting. For instance, King Arthur is just a boy when he tries to pull Excalibur from the stone. Everyone expects him to fail since he is just a young, powerless boy, except for Merlin who knows who Arthur truly is. As rightful king, Arthur is not just a young boy. Arthur is all of England—the people and the land. As the vector of England itself, Arthur has much more magnitude than one boulder would have, regardless of how big that boulder is. As the rightful king, the embodiment of all England, Arthur easily has enough magnitude to pull the sword from the stone.

Magnitude becomes a very interesting dramatic device when contrasts between the magnitudes of different vectors are drawn, especially between the protagonist and antagonist. How and when a weak vector gains more magnitude, or conversely a strong vector loses magnitude, can add to the suspense and/or anticipation of a literary or dramatic piece.

The revealing of a vector that had been disguised is a common technique in the Well-Made Play Structure to create excitement. Where the vector of greatest magnitude may be placed may also be hidden, disguised, or simply hard to reach for weak vectors. For instance, in the film *The Wizard of Oz,* the title character is considered to be the most powerful vector. However, Dorothy and her friends are presumably so weak that they have trouble reaching Oz. They are attacked by apple trees, confused by the paths, put to sleep by poppies, etc. Even when reaching Oz, they are told they are still too weak to share in the Wizard's power, and so must go and defeat the Wicked Witch. Returning triumphantly to Oz, they learn the Wizard is not so powerful and cannot help Dorothy. But then the most powerful vector is revealed—Dorothy has had it all along. The vector with the greatest power had not been recognized and so could not be used.

The forces of concern within literary and dramatic

works add or subtract their power through convergences with each other exactly in the manner specified by vector theory. Convergences, the types already identified by theatrical aesthetics, and their functions are described in the next chapter.

Chapter Four:

Convergences:

Rising Action—the Inciting Incident, Reversals, Complications, the Climax

Mathematicians, physicists, and engineers speak of the action lines of forces intersecting. Since the educated lay prefers more direct, concise, and succinct language, the common parlance term *convergence* is used in this book to mean the intersection of forces' action lines.

Convergences of vectors in literature and drama take a number of forms such as physical interactions—the characters, props, or locales touch each other wholly or in part; oral interactions—the characters tell each other things; written interactions—the characters give each other letters, telegrams, emails, and notes; sensory interactions like a locale that changes temperature or emits an odor, or special sound effects like the mysterious sound of a scythe. Ghost stories, fantasy stories, science fiction tales, etc. add to these forms dreams, hauntings, and other out-of-the ordinary manifestations of forces.

Every work of literature and drama must contain a convergence that is a summation of the vast majority of the vectors. This can be accomplished in two ways: either all, or nearly all, of the vectors individually converge at the same time and place, or a series of convergences consolidates the many vectors into a small number of major vectors which then will converge all together at the same time and place. Whichever way, the convergence that is comprised of the vast majority of the vectors is the climactic convergence—ordinarily known in aesthetics as the climax. Any few vectors that did not converge with the vast majority must converge after the climax, and all vectors must converge at the climactic convergence or immediately thereafter or be understood that they will converge in the very, very near future after the story's end, as it were. If there is no climax the work feels unfinished, and indeed, as engineers understand vector theory, a system will not be "concurrent" if all the vectors do not have their action lines intersect (Jenson and Chenoweth, 1983, p. 10)—no concurrency, no structure. If the vectors do not converge, they simply keep traveling along their course ways off into infinity, failing to finalize the form of the piece. Naturally, works that have only one convergence, the climactic one, tend to be very short. The puppet sketch of "Oh No Mr. Bill!" is such a piece. (This is a short, comic puppet play where a puppet sees a huge mallet looming, screams "Oh No Mr. Bill!" and is then flattened by the mallet.) Most works of literature and drama, however, make use of a carefully structured set of convergences, some of which are considered so important they are named.

The first such convergence that is termed in theatrical aesthetics is the inciting incident. Theatrical artists are quite aware that the opening exposition that so many works of literature use translates to the stage as a long-winded and dull speech that makes audiences restless. For most of theatrical history making an audience restless could be quite dangerous, for the audience, particularly the Gallery of the Gods (now more known by the French term *les enfants du paradis*), was wont to throw things at the actors as well as at each other. In order to prevent a restless audience from breaking out into a brawl (which was not unknown) theatrical artists realize it behooves them to have something very active and exciting occur on stage immediately. Shakespeare, for instance, used such inciting incidents as opening *Romeo and Juliet* with a street brawl; opening *Hamlet* with a ghost haunting soldiers on their guard post; opening *Macbeth* with witches brewing a spell; opening *Twelfth Night* with a ship wreck and a lord moaning over a lady; opening the *Taming of the Shrew* with some men playing a ribald prank on a drunk; opening *A Midsummer Night's Dream* with the revels of a wedding disrupted by quarrelling lovers; etc., etc.

The inciting incident consists of a convergence of some of the major vectors of the literary or dramatic piece to the detriment of the protagonist. The characters involved may not be the main characters; nevertheless, they as bodies propelled by vectors will establish what the salient forces at work in the piece are. For instance, in *Romeo and Juliet,* the brawl is between the Montagues and the Capulets, a feud vector, yet none of the main characters takes part. The brawl results in the death of a character so minor we never hear of him again, but the character is related to the second important vector—the Prince in his position as keeper of law and order. The brawl partly destroys the two vectors of the Prince (the death of the relative), and the feud vector of the Capulets and the Montagues.

In the inciting incident of *Hamlet*, only Hamlet, his friend Horatio, and Hamlet's ghostly father are present. Although they are all part of the same protagonistic vector, they individually are affected by differing vectors—and so the problem of the whole play is presented—the realm is threatened within and without. The kingdom may be attacked by Fortinbras, and a usurper has taken the Danish throne through murder. Hamlet must avenge his father's murder but the murder charge is based on a phantasm, not real evidence. In *Macbeth* the witches give Macbeth an illegal prophecy that will come true, but because it was not permissibly given, will spell his doom. The witches are minor characters and yet they are a powerful vector of the play because their charm sets all the forces into action.

In *Twelfth Night* we have the amusing inciting incident of a man who pines for a woman who openly loathes him juxtaposed with the excitement of the shipwrecking of the woman who will love him secretly. This inciting incident gives four major vectors: a spoiled woman who does not want the hero; a brave woman, the incognito heroine, who does want the hero; the thought-to-be-drowned brother of the heroine; and the hero who must decide whom he really wants. *The Taming of the Shrew*'s inciting incident is interesting in that it establishes the vector of a lord who uses sexual pranks to save people from self-destructive behavior. In *A Midsummer Night's Dream*, the inciting incident establishes the vectors of lovers trying to defy legally ordained matches. Only one set of lovers is missing from the scene, but that pair, Titania and Oberon will be of the same kind of vector—a woman refusing her legally approved mate.

Well crafted inciting incidents like Shakespeare's use the major vectors in the inciting incident to establish through their convergence the overall direction of the entire work. In *Romeo and Juliet* the direction is of the feud; in *Hamlet*, the direction is of revenge; in *Macbeth* the direction is of fate; in *Twelfth Night* it is of the confusion of love; in *The Taming of the Shrew* it is of sexual learning; in *A Midsummer Night's Dream* it is of ordained love. Each of these directions has two senses: feuds always involve two sides—two families; fate brings both fortune and ruin; revenge can be vengeance or an avenging; the confusion of love stems from loving both who is right and who is wrong for you; sexual learning teaches both to expect better (the drunk is to wake up in a wonderful bed instead of the smelly street) and to expect worse (Kate's many trials); ordained love brings joy if accepted and trouble if rejected.

The inciting incident, or inciting convergence, serves several important dramatic purposes. It grabs the audience's attention (and so is also called "a grabber"); it establishes the setting which is often the major locale vector; it establishes the antagonistic and protagonist forces in form of characters; it establishes what the goal or goals of the antagonistic and protagonistic forces are; it establishes what the major prop vector is if there is one; and it establishes what type of theatrical experience the production will be—tragedy, comedy, or whichever form of melodrama (drama, mystery, or thriller). Through establishing the major vectors and identifying the type of theatrical work the production will be, the inciting incident—at least in well-crafted works—suggests both the theme of the show and what the major events will be. The better crafted the theatrical work is, the more information the inciting incident will give.

For instance, Shakespeare's inciting convergence of King Lear with his three daughters, their husbands, Kent, and the whole court is so constructed as to: reveal clearly the protagonists and antagonists; establish the theme(s) of the play; sufficiently warn the audience the play will be a tragedy with a capital T; and to completely outline the major events of the play in a way that makes riveting theater. Three props are called for in the scene since they are specifically required by the lines (what the characters say): a map of England, a sword, and a crown. The map, the first prop called for, introduces the vector of England and that Lear intends to divide the kingdom. Right away the audience knows the splitting of such a powerful vector as England will cause disaster. The second prop called for, the sword, represents the warfare that will result from Lear's rash handling of his succession and his favoring of his less than worthy daughters, Goneril and Regan. The third prop called for, the crown, represents the central issue of the play—the question of who will succeed Lear as monarch.

The construction of the scene is so skillful, and the props are so organic to the scene, that their larger importance as signifying vectors is understated with the greatest finesse and subtlety. To the audience, the map has to be there because Lear is showing his daughters what their respective slices of England will be. The map seems to be an innocuous show-and-tell diagram, not a looming vector. Lear's pulling out his sword and nearly murdering his best friend shows Lear has a dangerous temper when roused, and also shows the depth of his hurt at his youngest daughter's refusal to say how much she loves him. Again, the sword seems be the expected accoutrement of a primitive, hot-tempered king, not a harbinger of things to come. The crown, which is a particularly interesting theatrical device because of the practical problem of who is to take it when Lear holds it out and who is to bear it off the stage at the end of the scene, also seems to be more an object of show rather than of deep meaning. (If ever I were to direct Lear, I would have Lear put the crown on his own head quickly after holding it out, and exit wearing it, to show that even though he "steps down" he has trouble completely relinquishing his rights as king.) In this manner of analyzing the scene for the major forces of the play, the importance of the props stands out and so suggests ways of handling the props, especially a particularly tricky one like the crown. (I will never forget the performance I saw where the crown was left rolling about on the stage after all the actors had exited for the next scene. When the actors re-entered, there was this crown on the floor that they kept knocking into and kicking about. Props must be dealt with, and better they be dealt with in a manner that helps to bring out the meaning of the play.)

Film also has a precise term for a convergence that acts as a means of establishing the important vectors. The *establishing shot* is usually a long shot that is used at the beginning of a scene to set the interrelationship between details to be shown in subsequent nearer shots (Reisz and Millar, 1968, p. 399). The "details" will be of character vectors (often doing something), prop vectors, or the locale vector, or any combination thereof. The point of the establishing shot is that the key elements—the important vectors—are converging, usually in an "oblique impact." Many films open with an establishing shot, but an establishing shot is frequently used at other points in the film when the importance of the coming more complete convergence is imminent.

After the inciting incident, the subsequent convergences of a literary or dramatic piece will take some basic or, as it is called in the theater," stock" forms. One form is that the protagonist meets with other protagonistic forces and is strengthened. The convergences between the protagonistic forces usually shift the direction of the main character vector, taking the form of new strategies. In mathematics this would be graphed, for instance, as a force moving up converging with a force moving to the right. The two forces combine to move upward towards the right; that is, diagonally rather than vertically like the first vector or horizontally like the second. The second form is of the antagonist meeting with the other antagonistic forces. Here, too, the vectors are strengthened but alter direction in terms of the behavior being shifted somewhat when the forces converge. How fully same-sense vectors converge will determine how much they strengthen each other and how much they influence each other's direction. If the same-sense vectors only "obliquely impact" each other, the magnitude will be strengthened and the direction altered to the degree of how much the vectors have converged. If it is a mild brushing, the effects will be smaller than those of a more thorough convergence.

The next forms of typical convergences were first described by Aristotle as "reversals" –reversals of fortune for the protagonist. The protagonist, or a positive character, prop, or location vector converges with the antagonist or a negative character, prop, or location vector. Depending on how fully the countering vectors converge, the vectors will either obliterate each other, or the stronger vector will obliterate the weaker one (though naturally in the middle of the work, the protagonist will not be obliterated because then the play would be over), or there will be an "oblique impact" where the harm to one or both vectors ranges from serious (but not immediately destructive) to mild depending on the degree of contact between the "bodies"—characters, props, and locale.

Another form of reversal is a character switching sides—an ally of the protagonist joining forces with the antagonist. This occurs because a character can be the foci of numerous vectors, and in a convergence with the antagonistic forces, an ally of the protagonist can have his or her positive vectors partially or completely destroyed so that only the character's negative vectors are left which are strengthened by the joining with the antagonist's negative vectors. In mystery and suspense stories, frequently the switching of sides is attributed to some kind of coercion or intimidation. In this case character has only positive vectors, but those vectors are of less magnitude than that of the antagonists' and so not only has the character lost magnitude in the convergence but faces the threat of having some crucial-to-his-or-her-life vector completely destroyed, such as a family member or livelihood. In adventures and comedies, the conversion is usually due to the character being persuaded that his or her best interests lie with the opposition. In this case, the character has both positive and negative vectors, and the joining of the negative vectors with the antagonist's negative vectors make the character more strongly negative.

A character being the foci of more than one vector can aid in creating anticipation and/or suspense. In some stories, the audience or reader already knows this is apt to happen, has been expecting this, and so is in a state of anticipation. For instance in the film 1943 Hollywood film *Shadow of a Doubt*, it is not as clear to the heroine as it is to the audience that her uncle is, indeed, a serial killer. For a time, the heroine only sees the positive sense vector of her uncle: he is her mother's favorite brother, a beloved member of the family. However, the uncle suffered an injury in childhood that gave him a demonic side, and it is this negative force of his personality the uncle is successful in hiding from the family. The audience expects the uncle to try to kill the heroine, and the film even shows him preparing a death trap for her. The audience anticipates the moment when the heroine will finally be convinced that her uncle is a murderer; the audience wonders what it will be that will convince her.

In mysteries, the audience will not be expecting the betrayal and will be put into a state of suspense. For instance, in Collins' *The Woman in White*, Miss Halcombe rescues her cousin from the insane asylum where the Count had hidden the cousin. Miss Halcombe brings her cousin to their uncle who refuses to recognize or can not recognize the cousin and throws the cousins out. The uncle upon whom they should have been able to count for protection puts them into a worse situation. In this case the uncle is again of the positive vector of head of the family. However, his position is not entirely secure. When the cousin has a son, it will be that son, and not the uncle, who is entitled to the monies and title of the estate. Therefore the uncle has an interest in the cousin being disposed of and so also has negative vectors driving his behavior. These types of plays of forces create "reversals" for the protagonist characters as well as creating anticipation and suspense.

Another type of convergence known to dramatic aesthetics is the *complication*. Complications can be reversals, but they can also be convergences that benefit the protagonist. Complications "complicate" the plot in that either a hitherto unknown vector appears to converge with the protagonist to his detriment or his advantage, or a known vector affects the protagonist in an unexpected way. When the vector is known, either its magnitude or its sense is not actually known, and the unknown quality results in the unexpected. For instance, a negative vector that is thought to be of little magnitude will converge with a positive vector, overpowering it, thus causing a surprising setback for the protagonist or his allies. Or, a positive vector will unexpectedly be unable to converge with (or refuse to converge with) the protagonist (a near miss) until it receives more magnitude from the protagonist. An obvious example of this is in *The Wizard of* Oz: the Wizard will not let Dorothy and her friends approach him too closely until they have obtained the Wicked Witch's broom.

Complications add interest value and/or excitement to the literary or dramatic work because of the unexpectedness of the resultant. Typically, complications in the form of reversals occur in the first part of a dramatic piece with complications that are to the protagonist's advantage occurring in the second because the reversals are new problems that hinder the protagonist and/or his allies' attempt to find a solution to their original problem while complications that are to the protagonist's advantage tend to be the solutions to their problems. The problems, of course, are some sort of loss of magnitude which prevents the protagonistic forces from traveling along their course, preventing character-vectors from achieving their objectives, and solutions are basically various types of gains in magnitude that allow for the protagonistic vectors to travel along their direction, allowing the character-vectors to achieve their objectives.

If the tale is to end happily, then any reversals in the protagonist's fortunes must be put to rights. Here again there are some typical techniques. One is that a positive character vector who was intimidated or otherwise overpowered by the antagonist converges with something or someone that is of a positive vector, and so is able to come to the aid of the protagonist. This can be that the protagonist's allies have been able to unite and with their united strength converge with the protagonist to strengthen the protagonist. The other frequently used technique is that a positive vector, usually a prop or a character, unexpectedly comes to the aid of the protagonist. In Moliere's *Tartuffe*, all seems lost for Orgon, but the king's envoy speaks up at the last minute saving the day. Representing all the power of the king, the envoy has more than enough magnitude to set all problems to rights.

Convergences are also used for specific effects for the different types of literary and dramatic pieces. A structural device commonly used in comedies, particularly in farce, is to take a wide variety of vectors and force them to converge until the sheer number of countering vectors being forced into convergence results in them all being divided again. For instance in the Marx brothers' film *A Night at the Opera* there is a famous *bit* of many people filling up a closet-sized cabin. Each of the people has a very different position in life and came to be in the cabin room for very different reasons, but regardless, they continue to conduct their business in the tiny cabin in a very matter-of-fact way. More and more people fill the cabin room until the audience can not believe so many people can fit in there. Eventually the miniscule room becomes so crammed with people that when one more person tries to enter, it explodes and the people go flying out of it.

In *A Midsummer Night's Dream*, Puck through trickery tries to get all the lovers together, but instead creates worse mayhem. In tragedy, every convergence has the effect of furthering the destruction of the protagonist. In mysteries and thrillers, convergences are frequently to effect surprise either through unexpected convergences, an expected convergence with an unexpected vector, or an expected convergence with an expected body (character, prop, or locale) having an unexpected resultant (due to the body's being influenced by a different vector than expected).

In science fiction, the convergences are with "aliens," which means that interest and excitement are created by figuring out just exactly what the qualities—magnitude, direction, and sense— of the alien-vectors are. In romances, the majority of the convergences are to show that the hero does indeed have all the hoped-for vectors the heroine wants in a man. The hero may not have them all at first and so must acquire them, or he can have the vectors but they can be temporarily masked by overriding negative vectors. In the end though, the hero must have all the requisite vectors with sufficient magnitude and then the hero and heroine climactically converge, explicitly so in the more erotically oriented romances.

The theatrical term of *rising action* is one of those terms that has been intuitively understood and defined loosely as all the actions or events of a theatrical piece that contribute to the audience's building excitement. The inciting incident is intended to create a burst of excitement and the various reversals, complications, and other events are all intended to maintain the audience's interest, to raise the audience's excitement level, and to direct that excitement towards the understanding of the production's ultimate communication. How rising action achieves this, and achieve this it must, is not explained except in the form of comparisons being drawn between different works as examples of techniques to create rising action, or the simple assertion of the skilled professional that "Yes, that will work."

While examples are useful for understanding, they are not concisely definitive, and while relying on the judgment of a professional is also fruitful *that* is not one-hundred percent sure at all times. Vector theory, however, is definitive and consistently accurate in every circumstance. So, when the actions or events of literature and drama are regarded as the converging of forces, then excitement is understood to be garnered through an estimation of magnitude; interest is garnered by the creation of new or reorientation of established behavior through convergence (alterations in sense); and communication of the production's message is reliably achieved by the establishment of the vectors' directions. Having a system of analysis is much more effective than trial and error, particularly for a profession where there are strict deadlines and time is money.

In film, rising action is understood as a chain of plot points, also known as action points or transition points, that are the turning points of the action. Indeed, what is known as a *beat sheet* (from the idea of beats from The Method) is often drawn up; a beat sheet is a list charting a story's major plot points (Wilen and Wilen, 2000, p. 21).

Interesting, the film terminology is closer to the engineering language of a convergence in that the action lines are coming together at points.

Eventually, the rising action reaches its pinnacle in the climax. The salient forces must converge at the same time and place to form the climax. This can take the form of many characters meeting at the same vector location, or it can take the form of only two vectors, one positive and one negative, coming together at the same time and place. In the case of only two vectors meeting, each vector has accumulated magnitude from previous convergences with same-sense vectors. The more forces present or the greater the magnitude of the forces present at the climactic convergence the more exciting the climax will be for the reader or audience. Convergences form the different events of a literary or dramatic work. The structuring of convergences so that a final convergence, a climax, can and does occur is what gives each tale the dramatic shape it must have to be a fully realized tale, a satisfying work of art. Yet what vectors and how many vectors converge and how many convergences there are is uniquely determined by each storyteller, which is why there are potentially limitless artistic creations.

Chapter Five:
Lulls and Falling Action

In theatrical aesthetics, lulls are the moments of quiet between the moments of action. Since the moments of action are the moments of forces' convergence, the lulls are the periods of time when the resultant of the convergence is expressed. Time is needed for the audience to observe the direction, magnitude, and sense of the new force.

The time given to a resultant must be in keeping with the resultant's magnitude. The bigger the magnitude of the resultant of a convergence the longer it will take the audience to absorb it. If the magnitude is immense, the audience will think that the show is over since so much time must be given to the resultant. This is why each major event in the theater must be "topped" by the next major event. Every convergence must have a resultant of greater magnitude than the preceding convergence. A convergence that generates a vector of great magnitude can precede a convergence that has a resultant of much smaller magnitude, but the smaller convergence must be part of a series of small convergences with the summation of their resultants being greater than that of the one, big convergence.

For instance, in a fireworks show, a huge explosion of light is then followed by a series of small, quickly paced little explosions of light which in total effect lasts slightly longer than the one big explosion. A really good fireworks artist makes a pause before setting off the last of the little explosions with the last being slightly bigger than its fellows. A series of small convergences with a collective of resultants which together are a little larger than a preceding convergence of big vectors tells the audience that there will be more major events, that the big resultant was not the last of the production. Through the structuring of the convergence of vectors and their resultants theatrical presentations are given their dramatic shape. Lulls, as the time needed to express resultants, are integral to the art of the drama.

In the theater there are specific moments when actors routinely observe a lull. One of the most common is not generally seen by the public since it occurs at auditions. Actors normally do a prepared piece at auditions; at the end of the piece the actress will *hold*, which means she freezes in position for a moment right after delivering the final words of her piece *to hold the moment*. This allows the mood of the piece to naturally take its effect on the audience, in this case the casting committee or director, and eases the audience from the reality of the piece to the reality of everyday life. Similarly in performances, actors will *hold* for the audience to fully absorb the comedy of a line or the pathos of a line. Depending on the depth of meaning, the *hold* will either be very short or significantly long; for instance a double-entendre may have several layers of humor requiring a longer *hold*. Indeed, the audience may not at first "get the joke" and needs a lengthy *hold*; in such cases, at first the audience may be silent and then reacts with building laughter which crescendos as audience appreciation of the layers of meaning rises. Sometimes the *hold* is not for the audience to grasp the meaning, but is used because the mood created by the action is such a pleasant sensation that the audience wants a moment to savor the feeling. Vectorially speaking, the audience simply enjoys the emotions associated with a particular resultant—the new force—and needs a moment to fully experience or observe it.

Holding the moment also is used in The Method when there is a beat change where the new beat is significantly different from the former beat. The actress will make a "transition" which means that she will *hold* for a bit to allow the first beat to finish its expression and then she will ease into the movement and words of the next beat. Such transitions grip the audience's attention because they allow the audience to absorb the resultant of the first beat and anticipate the next beat. An example of such a beat change—two very different beats coming one right after the other—is in *Richard III* when the Crown Prince says, "I do not like the Tower of any place. Did Julius Caesar build that place my lord?" (III, i). In the first sentence the child is afraid of the Tower because he knows people are routinely sent there to await execution. The audience knows the child is about to be executed. In the second sentence, the child is relating himself to Julius Caesar since Caesar was a great emperor and the child is expecting to be coronated and so could become an emperor himself. In the first sentence the child is afraid, afraid of the future; in the second sentence he is bravely looking forward to the future. The pair of sentences are very much what children do: speak simply, and try to put a positive look to a scary circumstance so they can endure it. The child's subtext, his fear of being executed to his move into courage, must be made clear for the pathos of the scene to have its full effect; thus a transition in the form of a lengthy pause followed by different body language is a means of establishing the difference between the first sentence and the second.

The Kabuki Theater has a special term for some specific lulls. A "*mie*" is a stylized pose used at key moments, such as to close a scene; the *mie* represents the effect the action has had upon the actor/character (Ernst, 1956, p. 178 & 199). Interestingly, *mie* themselves are said to have a climax (Ernest, 1956, p. 112) which is the crossing of one eye (Ernest, 1956, p. 178) once the stance is made. When the eye is crossed, the whole pose is held for a time creating the striking moment. In the Kabuki, "it is not the blow itself which is important but the effect of it upon him [the character/actor]" (Ernst, 1956, p. 199). Indeed *mie* are "the ultimate physical expression toward which all Kabuki movement tends" (Ernst, 1956, p.

178). This reflects that still moments in theater are recognized as sometimes superceding action in importance. Method actors, when praising a production, will say "I love that moment when," referring to one of the *holds* or other expressions of a resultant.

Like the *mie* in Kabuki, which is used to finish a scene or highlight an important moment, film also has special techniques for the same purposes. "Every editor knows that the simple act of cutting from a general shot to a close up adds an important dimension or significance to any scene" (Dmytryk, 1984, p. 73). Usually the camera "holds" for a moment on the close up, and this, by establishing the resultant, creates the sense of significance. Long shots also can and are used to establish information and drama (Dmytryk, 1984, p. 74). Similarly, the wide-angle lens is used to provide greater illusion of depth or dimension to accentuate important moments (Dmytryk, 1984, p. 84). The narrow-angle lens with its shallow depth of focus can be used to sharply focus on the eyes while leaving the area of the ears and nose softer, calling attention to the expression of the eyes; this too is a technique for establishing resultants. "One of the great advantages of the medium [film] is that there are so many techniques which if properly and creatively used, can reach beyond each performer's own resources to make a film's inhabitants more dynamic and dramatically effective, while still keeping them human and real" (Dmytryk, 1984, p. 89).

Lulls which are used to *hold the moment*, such as a transition that comes between two sentences in a speech, allow the audience to savor a just-finished speech or absorb the significance of an actor's expression are quite short and momentary. However, lulls can be fairly lengthy, encompassing some "business" (a specific set of actions like a character settling down to sleep) as they express the resultant. Such longer moments are often thought of as *sustained moments*. There are entire speeches and songs which express the resultant and so can be classed as sustained moments in that they are sustaining a specific mood. A lull, in the theater, is thought of as a moment of quiet while the sustained moments, which tend to be richly interesting, are when a dramatic activity must be lengthened to emphasize the importance of the moment.

Lulls and closures of scenes often are expressed as a *bit of business—a bit*—a small, but important piece of the play like a speech or a scripted activity like an embrace. A bit of business, a small activity, is developed by an actress for those times when she is onstage but her character is not the focus, or when a transition is needed between events and none has been supplied by the script (which is a frequent occurrence), or when a scene ends and characters are left on stage with no scripted lines (another common occurrence). As the audience is not expected to leave the theater except for the intermission and the end of the show, the audience's attention has to be maintained throughout. The quiet of lulls and the transitions expressed by bits of business help maintain audience attention by providing pauses for the audience to rest from the excitement of convergences and reflect upon and absorb the resultants of the convergences.

Resting a moment from the excitement of convergences is important, or the audience's emotional reactions can get away from the control of the actors. The great comic actor and playwright of the English stage, Noel Coward said, "I believe that all acting is a question of control, the control of the actor of himself, and through himself of the audience" (*Great Acting*, p. 165); "if you lose yourself you're liable to lose them [the audience]" (*Great Acting*, p. 166). This must not happen because it diverts the audience from the communication of the production. It is difficult to regain control of the audience once control has been lost. If the loss of control is too long, historically the audience could become quite dangerous. Audiences have been known to become unpleasantly rowdy, unruly, and even riotous. When the actors do not have control over the emotions of the audience, the audience's attention is not focused on the events and meaning of the production. When the audience's attention is broken, they cease to enjoy the show, or with well-behaved audiences, enjoy the show less than they would if they continued to be captivated. Edith Evans, another great of the English stage, also spoke of this need to keep control of the audience: "Don't be delighted when they scream at you and think it's awfully funny; you should be upset because they have no business to scream. They should laugh but only if you want them to laugh. When they start getting out of hand you must calm them down" (*Great Acting*, p. 130).

Lulls in the theater also assist in establishing the rhythm of a production in the manner that rests do for music. As an art form that is temporal, the structuring of events means that there will be at times swiftly occurring actions, "pregnant pauses" that herald a punch line, slowly unfolding actions, *holds* after important speeches, sustained moments, and closures of scenes, acts, and the work itself. How these different uses of time are structured give a sense of rhythm and movement to the production. If the moments of resultants— the holds, sustained moments, and closure of scenes and acts—are too long they will make the production lag; too short and the audience will tire.

In the theater, the audience "suspends disbelief," accepting the world of the production as "real." Indeed, all cultures throughout history have considered their form of theater realistic (Clay, 1951, p. v). Readers also will enter the world of the tale they read, even to the point of feeling themselves to be inside the story, vicariously experiencing it (Segel, 1995, pp. 61-78). The tendency is so common among people who love to read fiction that psychologists have termed such readers "immersed readers" (Rolf Zwaan, e-mail, Aug. 13, 14:40; and 28, 2002). Interruptions jolt the audience and reader out of the reality of the play or tale, and lags bore the audience or reader out of the reality of the literary or dramatic piece.

Historically, in the theater, if the Gallery of the Gods

has its attention on the play broken, that portion of the audience is apt to throw things at the stage, at each other, and at hapless audience members in the balconies below them. American high school audiences tend to follow in this tradition (unknowing that they are following a tradition) when, during a film, they throw their popcorn at the screen when a lull does not express the resultant but is an unbelievable insertion. This danger of being pelted by something has induced many theater artists to make sure something is always happening, like in the film *King Kong*, to be sure of maintaining audience interest. Yet, a lull that is in theater terms "organic"—grows out of the action—is highly satisfying to audiences, and this is because such a lull is the expression of a resultant.

Therefore, if the lull after the convergence does not demonstrate the resultant of the convergence, the audience or reader will feel jarred into disbelief. That is, the *suspension of disbelief*—the acceptance of the reality of the events of the theatrical or literary piece—will be broken. This explains why musical theater will either exasperate its audiences or delight them. In a musical, an important action will occur and then the characters sing and usually dance. In good musicals, such as *West Side Story*, the song is the resultant and so is an organic part of show. The song and dance pleases the audience by the beauty of the expression of the resultant's magnitude, direction, and sense. In bad musicals, the action is simply stopped—interrupted—by a song. This frustrates and annoys the audience because the needed resultant of the convergence is replaced by a (usually sappy) song which does not demonstrate all or even any of the new vector's qualities. In some musicals, like *Godspell,* the song will be the convergence itself combined with its resultant, and this is, of course, very satisfying for audiences. The song "Day by Day" encompasses the convergence of a devoted follower with Jesus and the resultant of that convergence. The song is full of long, sustained notes giving the qualities of the resultant of the follower/Jesus convergence: sense— love (positive); direction— the course of the singer's entire life; and magnitude—full, powerful devotion.

Perhaps the most famous lull is Hamlet's "to be or not to be" speech (Act III, scene i). During that speech, Hamlet is secretly watched by the audience and characters, but they do not interfere with him and he believes himself alone and so he thinks aloud of the different vectors moving him. The vectors represented by Claudius (usurper of the throne), Pollonius (court advisor), Ophelia (love), the audience (as the people of Denmark), and Hamlet (various vectors including rightful heir creating internal conflict within him) converge in an oblique impact to find Hamlet talking to himself.

Once the transformation has been clearly established the vectors need to move towards another convergence. If no more convergences occur, then the show is over. The less time there is between convergences the more quickly paced the work will be. Too many convergences coming in too fast of a succession can tire the reader or audience, and so occasional, longer lulls are called for because they allow the reader or audience to absorb the establishment of the newly directed vectors. In general, for both theatrical and literary pieces, if lulls last longer than it takes to convey what the transformed force is, the lulls will cause interest in the work to fall.

Literature is also a temporal art, but the greater length of novels means that while there will be some similarities to the theater as to when resultants occur and how they are handled, there will also be some striking differences. Before the advent of TV and radio, short stories were designed to be of a length that a person could read without feeling the need to look up—an hour or so of reading time. Similarly, novel chapters ended at "good stopping places" when a reader would be expected to be tired. Novel chapters tended to end with a chapter climax and a chapter denouement. Until the second half of the previous century, people tended to work very long hours and so needed to be able to set down a book for the night, but they should also want to pick it up again later. Thus, a chapter needed to "feel finished" on one level, but on another, it had to create curiosity for what or how things were to occur. The feeling of being finished comes from closure; some set of vectors have met with their final convergence resulting in a new force that moves off into infinity.

For an act end or chapter end, secondary or minor vectors will have their final convergence to create a resultant which gives a sense of closure. At the end of the novel or theatrical production, the main vectors will have their final convergence and the resultant of the climactic convergence gives the sense of closure. With chapter and act end climactic convergences, minor vectors need to have a final convergence for a sense of closure while the resultants of the major vectors' convergences have to have enough interest value that the reader would want to find out what happens to the newly directed vectors. Also the chapter and act resultants do distance the reader— that is how closure works—but the distancing is to a smaller degree than occurs in the denouement. If the reader is distanced from the story too much, the reader, of course, will not return to the story; the audience will not bother with the rest of show.

However, within the body of the chapter or story, lulls and *bits* are handled differently than they are for a theatrical production. The reader is expected to put down the book periodically, even frequently. In contrast with the theater, any savoring of moments or ruminations of the events that occurred for the written story are done by the reader when he or she chooses to look up from the book to ruminate for a moment or even when the reader sets the book aside for awhile. Accepting that the reader will look up or set aside the book, there are two basic ways lulls and bits are handled in literature which are different from the theater. On the one hand, since many novels of previous centuries sought to instruct, and the reader is expected, perhaps even encouraged, to ponder what the novel says, long passages of philosophy or moralizing—which would be intolerable for an audience—are satisfying and interesting for a reader. Thus lulls and *bits* in novels can be extremely long, being more of an essay than a creative sequence.

For instance, the novel *Moby Dick* has three chapters on how whales are depicted in woodcuts and other types of renderings; obviously that discussion is cut entirely from film versions of the novel. Similarly, in *Jane Eyre*, a full page of Christian ethos is given at the end of chapter six as the resultant of the convergence between Jane and Helen Burns, with the sermon finishing in Helen's silent musing. Through Helen's musings, the reader is encouraged to also reflect on the Christian teachings just given, and even to re-read them. A small convergence then occurs, when another busy-body child threatens to get Helen in trouble if Helen does not do some small task. This sends Helen away, leaving the reader with the wish of following her; thus, the chapter skillfully imbues the reader with the Christian vector that Helen embodies. To contrast this length of time that a resultant is allowed to be expressed in literature with lengths or resultants for the stage, the rule of thumb is that it takes two to three minutes to read aloud a page, and so Helen's speech lasts about three minutes. Audiences tend to find that long for a speech; the speeches in Shakespeare's plays average about a minute and a half—fully *half* the length of Helen's speech.

Although the speeches of the stage are shorter, making for shorter denouements to end acts and shorter lulls within acts, before the 1900's audiences did, like readers, like to have particularly meaningful resultants repeated. So, just as a reader may stop and re-read Helen's discourse on Christian values, so too performers did, at the urging of the audience, stop and repeat a speech or song. In the theater the repeating of a *bit* was known as *making points* with five points (the audience demanding the speech or song repeated five times) being the maximum that would occur. Although some of the *bits* the audiences wanted repeated were the apexes of the convergences, the *bits* would have also included the resultant of the convergence. Many favorite *bits* showed both the moment of convergence and the transformation the convergence effected. Even with the *points*, the repeated *bits* are shorter for audiences than they are for readers; likewise for lulls.

The other difference between literary and dramatic pieces is that lulls are absolutely essential for dramatic pieces; otherwise audiences become fatigued. A fatigued audience is an inattentive, squirming audience that wants to go home. In contrast to this, in literature for the last half century or so, not giving a reader a chance to catch his or her breath is often accounted a virtue and the work is described as "a real page turner." Lengthy lulls tend to cause the modern reader to toss the book aside permanently, so the resultants of the convergences lead directly to new convergences without giving the reader pause to think. Even chapter divisions are not restful; the reader is impelled to keep reading with the reader's assertion of "I couldn't put it down" being a high accolade. One means of propelling the reader on into the next chapter is accomplished by ending the chapter at the moment of the chapter's climax, without giving the resultant. Thus, the reader feels the need to know what happens as a result of the climax and jumps right into the next chapter. In the theater, television series are notorious for doing this, especially with the "season finale."

The falling action, or denouement, of a literary or theatrical piece is also a resultant. It is the resultant of the climactic convergence, the climax. The denouement creates for the audience or reader the final sensation of a satisfying finish— closure. Closure accomplishes three things: it confirms the work is over by using language of finality; it distances the reader or audience from work; and it directs the final force of the work either away from the reader or audience directly (the hero rides off into the sunset) or indirectly from the reader or audience's conscious into their subconscious ("and our little lives are rounded with a sleep").

In the theater it is observed that the last few minutes of the play or film—the denouement—is the most crucial part of the work in that it leaves the final impression; it is what the audience walks away with. The beginning of the work can be weak; the work as a whole can be uneven in quality, but if the finish is satisfying, the audience will be happy with the production and will go home having accepted the message of the production.

The form that the closure takes will depend upon what type of convergence the climax was. For instance, when a direct impact destroys the main characters, the place of convergence, and any significant prop, either the audience is purged of the emotions the work created in them, allowing for a catharsis, or the forces will return to the order they were in at the beginning of the piece when presumably they were in balance. In the latter case, the work will reestablish the balance of forces present at the beginning, and the audience or reader will feel pleasantly satisfied.

For instance, there was a *Star Trek* episode about an individual who could manipulate time and by doing so had created a time-line where his wife died. In an effort to bring her back to life, he continued to manipulate time, only to create more and more horrors for other people. At last the Federation characters were able to outwit him and destroy his time machine, thereby destroying everything, but the original balance, the time when the wife was still alive, comes fully back into being. The famous comic science-fiction film, *Dr. Strangelove*, ends with the complete and utter destruction of the whole world in a nuclear holocaust. The audience is able to endure this horrific end because the film is a farce, and the nature of farce is the humor of extremes. Nothing is left; the audience or reader experiences a warning of the earth's real possibility of finality with the warning given in a palatable but memorable form.

As Aristotle first theorized, a climax which is a direct impact that destroys all can give the audience a catharsis—a complete purge of emotion which cleanses them. Catharsis can be explained as the audience identifying with or sharing the effects of the forces represented upon the stage (or in the story read); since these vectors are obliterated by their convergence they are also obliterated in the audience or reader. Thus the audience member or reader feels purged—they have been. Whether the complete destruction results in a return to the original balance, gives a warning of finality, or serves as a catharsis, the audience or reader is satisfyingly disengaged from the literary or dramatic work.

Most works, however, do not end with complete obliteration; a resultant force is created from the climax which forms the denouement. When the literary or dramatic piece has been constructed in such a way that the protagonistic forces are strongest, then the finish of the piece, the denouement, the resultant, will be positive, up-beat, of a positive sense. If the antagonistic forces are strongest, then the resultant force will be of the essential quality of the antagonistic forces—negative and downbeat. *Immersed readers* and engrossed audiences are usually actively assessing the magnitude of the various vectors and actively identifying the types of vectors presented. Assessing the magnitude is part of what creates excitement in the piece; the discovery of great magnitude makes for great excitement. Identifying the vectors occurs because the audience or reader wants to identify with the protagonists and so judges which are sympathetic characters and which are not, and to what degree. From their very immersion in the work, readers and audience members are expecting resultants that are in keeping with their appraisal of the vectors.

This is most readily apparent in mysteries and thrillers where a puzzle is being presented and part of the satisfaction for the reader or audience is the figuring out of the puzzle. The resultants of the internal convergences focus the vectors into new, more directed vectors, giving the reader and audience member a clear idea of where the forces are moving. Therefore, by the time the climax occurs, the readers and audience members have a specific idea of what the climax's resultant should be. The dramatic or literary piece has engaged the reader's or audience's emotions to build up expectation. The denouement then must satisfy this emotionally built expectation by consisting of a resultant that is in keeping with the expectation that has been created, and the denouement must provide closure by releasing the audience or reader from the pent-up emotion. By the time of the climax, the reader or audience is hoping, expecting to feel a certain way at the end of the story or show because of the very immersion in which the successful dramatic or literary work has absorbed reader's or audience's attention. Further, the fulfillment of the expectation must also resolve the feelings invoked by the work; this is what the closure of the denouement does.

There have been works that end at the climax; Ibsen's *Ghosts* and *A Doll's House* are probably the most famous. *Ghosts* ends with the mother caught at the moment of decision of whether to give poison to her son who is in the last stages of a venereal disease as he requested when he was *compos mentis*. *A Doll's House* ends with the climactic slam of a door as Nora walks out on her husband and family. Although modern audiences are accepting of these endings, Ibsen's audiences found them so startlingly radical as to be offensive. When *Ghosts* was first published almost all the copies sent to Norway from Copenhagen were returned unsold (Lamm, 1952, p. 107); critics in England called the play, "Garbage and offal" ("Ghosts and Gibberings," 1891); and Ibsen was often "labeled 'dull, no playwright, poor artist,' and so on" (Clay, 1956, p. 65). "The profoundly serious and fearless mind of the great playwright had constructed a reality which, when thrust before the less serious and certainly less courageous minds of the public, gave them an almost traumatic experience" (Clay, 1956, p. 66). As Lawson notes (1960 p. 178) the climax of a play "gives the fullest expression to the laws of reality as the playwright conceives them. ...The climax is the concrete realization of the theme in terms of an event." Thus, Ibsen presented his audiences with a reality so new as to be threatening, and he ended both *Ghosts* and *A Doll's House* at the moment of greatest impact without showing the resultant force of that impact. Not only does Ibsen leave the two plays without clear-cut resolutions, he purposely leaves them at the moment of their greatest question. While Ibsen's original audiences were so shocked by his themes and so angered by the lack of resolution to *Ghosts* and *A Doll's House* that they found those two plays unwholesomely unrealistic, contemporary Western audiences appreciate the pertinence of the themes to their own lives and find in Nora's door slam and Mrs. Alving's dilemma an implied resolution.

What was happening with Ibsen's plays was that he was taking part in social reform by demanding that his audiences consider situations and perspectives at odds with social dictates. As with Artaud's Theater of Cruelty and the "Happenings" of the 1960's, theater that is concerned with social reform usually reforms through providing shocks to the audience. The on-stage nudity in the musical *Hair* certainly had its shock value. Most creators of fiction and theater, however, are concerned not with shocking people with a problem, as Ibsen did, or shocking people with the true nature of reality, as in the nudity of *Hair*, or shocking people to create a catharsis of cruelty to purge them of cruelty, as Artaud sought to do, but with showing how current problems can be transformed into a more utopic world.

Shakespeare spoke of how the feuds between families only kill their young people, but it is the love of the young people that can bring families together (*Romeo and*

Juliet); he spoke of how the most corrupt of tyrants can be brought down through the unity of factions in harmony (*Richard III*); and he spoke too of how a nation torn asunder through selfishness and greed can be restored through love and loyalty (*King Lear*). Shakespeare's messages are no less profound or moving for providing an answer to a society's most disturbing questions. This does not mean to say Shakespeare is superior for providing resolutions and Ibsen inferior for shocking audiences, but that each literary and dramatic artist can so construct his or her work to either shock or provide resolution according to their artistic vision. Vector theory elucidates what technique is being used and why audiences react as they do to those techniques.

While works about social reform may either shock audiences or provide a transformative resolution, genre works, such as lighter, comic plays and genre literature have as part of their appeal the promise of an expected outcome. When this outcome is not met—a comic piece has a dark end, for instance—the audience can feel "had," or worse, "burned," and instead of feeling satisfied and renewed feels angered. If the audience or reader feels tricked or betrayed in that the expectations they formed during their involvement with the literary or dramatic piece were not fulfilled, they will not accept the message of the dramatic or literary work. In Ibsen's case, he was of liberal enough mind that he saw the coming course of social events and wrote of them in *A Doll's House*, and he expressed in *Ghosts* the deeper individual torments established social mores can cause. Ibsen's messages in these two plays now meet with audience and reader approbation. The finish of each play is still somewhat of a shock, but rings true and now satisfies audiences as the correct resultant of the plays' forces.

The denouement, then, as the final expression of the literary or dramatic work's theme or message will be important as part of establishing a work as a piece of enduring artistry or a piece of shallow glossiness that will pass into oblivion. For instance, the majority of Shakespeare's plays endure because they are of themes that arise for every generation: the difficulty of communication between parents and children (*Romeo and Juliet, King Lear*); the need to know one's self to be successful in love (*Twelfth Night*); how suspicion can destroy all that is dear to one (*Othello, Hamlet*); how political intrigue that is based on lust for power destroys nations (*King Lear, Hamlet*).

The one play that stands out as great but that has fallen out of favor is *The Taming of the Shrew*. For most of the play, the romp of a trickster paired with a shrew is amusing. However, when Kate finishes the play with a statement of how women need to be subservient to men the play ceases to be timeless in its appeal. If the final speech is cut, then the play feels unfinished and also ceases to be Shakespeare's statement. If it is neither cut nor replaced, it aggravates modern audiences. The denouement rings false to modern audiences and so sours the comedy. The resultant of *The Taming of the Shrew* draws from the force of Petruchio's taking control of Kate (male dominance) to make her submissive. However, if the force of benevolent trickery—Petruchio tricking Kate out of her unpleasant behavior by proving to her that she is loved—is chosen as the main vector (the power of humor to liberate love), then, instead of a submissive woman, Kate could become a fellow trickster with her husband who helps others become happier by playing practical jokes on them. She would then in the final scene play some tricks on the men who bully their wives to the amusement and glee of Petruchio. Shakespeare chose the theme of the rightness of male supremacy over the theme of the power of humor to liberate love, even though until the last scene the theme of the power of humor to liberate love is actually the more prevalent one. By choosing a socially accepted theme (the rightness of male dominance) as his final statement rather than presenting a theme of a human truth (as he does in his other plays) Shakespeare consigns *The*

Taming of the Shrew to the ranks of a troublesome play.

This suggests that when the resultant of works of literature and drama create denouements that speak to individual truths, as Ibsen's *Ghosts* and Shakespeare's other plays do, rather than socially determined ethos, then they inspire the reader or audience with that sense of self-knowledge newly acquired that touches and changes who the reader or audience member is. When a work of fiction is good enough to encourage the reader to be "an involved reader" or when in the theater the audience is "sitting on the edge of their seats, playing the parts themselves" the denouement leaves the reader or audience with the Welsh miner's reaction to Edith Evan's playing of Medea: "This play is for us. It kindles a fire.'" As Evans commented, "And what more do you want to do in the theatre but kindle a fire?" (*Great Acting*, 1967, p. 60).

Closure, then, is vital to the construction of literary and dramatic art in that it forms the means through which the meaning of the work is internalized by the reader or audience member so that the change of being the experience of the literary or dramatic artwork was meant to effect can be effected.

Specific techniques of closure have been developed in literature and drama, some of which are culturally oriented. Poems will normally end with a last word that gives a sense of finality, such as the word *end* or the word "death." Fairy tales of the English speaking countries end with "And everybody lived happily ever after" while Spanish fairy tales often end with the saying *"Colorin colorado: este cuento se ha acabado"* ("Colored pencils are red: this story is finished"). The Spanish saying is particularly explicit in referring to drawing a red line to mark the end of the story. American tales often end with the cowboy or hero riding off into the sunset while Irish fairy tales often end with the hero and heroine turning into swans and then flying around the lake three times. Novels and theatrical works frequently finish with a statement that sums up the theme or makes a comment of some kind about an aspect of the book or play. Some of the most famous of these are: "It is a far, far better thing I do now than I have ever done before" (*A Tale of Two Cities*); "Tomorrow is another day" (*Gone With the Wind*); and "God bless us everyone" (*A Christmas Carol*). Like the last word of a poem, a novel will often finish with an image of leave-taking or finality: *Lady Chatterley's Lover*—"John Thomas says good-night to lady Jane, a little droopingly, but with a hopeful heart"; *One Hundred Years of Solitude*—"because races condemned to one hundred years of solitude did not have a second opportunity on earth"; *Fathers and Sons*—"However passionate, sinful and rebellious the heart hidden in the tomb, the flowers growing over it peep at us serenely with their innocent eyes; they speak to us not only of eternal peace, of the vast repose of 'indifferent' nature; they tell us, too, of everlasting reconciliation and of life which has no end." Film and theater also use the techniques of literature, but the salient forms of closure are visual devices such as special camera effects in film, the pointed exit of a main character, or, in live theater, the lights dim and go out.

Chapter Six
Vector Theory and Established Aesthetic Theories of Plot

The majority of the dramatic aesthetic theories have focused on a particular area of concern: Aristotle with the description of plots; neoclassicists with believability in plot construction; Scribe with the nuts and bolts of a workable plot formula; Delsarte with scientific principles being applied to the actor's art; Stanislavsky's Method with how an actor sustains dramatic reality moment by moment; Artaud with the metaphysically therapeutic value of theater; conflict theory with the dynamic interaction between characters; and metaphorical analysis with unifying the elements of a dramatic production into a greater or transcendent meaning. These seeming disparate theories are frequently used in concert with each other and are not seen as conflicting approaches. The reason why a neoclassical script can have a Method production to the delight of its modern audience, or why the Delsarte System interjected into a script built upon conflict theory makes for a gripping production is that these theories are analogous to facets of vector theory. Each theory has direct correspondences with vector theory, emphasizing different aspects of theatrical concern. Each dramatic theory, in other words, corresponds to a different part of vector theory.

Aristotle's (found in Wietz, 1970, p. 685) observation that plot is a structure of incidents corresponds directly to vector theory in so far as the study of statics, a basis of engineering, provides a means towards creating structures. Aristotle's further observation that any displacement or removal of any of its parts makes a piece of drama (he specifies tragedies) seem disjointed and incomplete is also in keeping with vector theory in that the resultant desired by the playwright or literary author cannot be obtained without specific forces being drawn together in convergence. A specific resultant will require the convergence of forces of certain magnitude, certain sense, and certain direction. If any significant forces are missing at the climactic convergence, the resultant will not occur or will be other than the author or playwright intends. Aristotle also noted that the "complication" leads to a certain point where a change occurs, a "turning point from good or bad fortune" and this fits as simple language for what vector theory describes exactly. The complications are the convergences between some of the different sense forces prior to the climax, and the changes are the convergences' resultants where the forces are transformed by their convergences into new forces. Aristotle's "reversals" and "recognition scenes" are convergences between different sense forces for the former, and convergences between same sense vectors for the latter. The protagonist will be thrown off course or lose strength (or both) by meeting with the antagonist; the protagonist will be propelled more strongly along his course or directed more accurately towards it through meetings with other protagonistic forces in the form of other characters, objects, or locales. Although Aristotle felt that the complications and denouement "turn upon surprises" (found in Weitz, 1970, p. 690), it is actually the alteration and creation of forces that provide interest and excitement whether they be surprises or not.

Aristotle's concept of catharsis, the purging of negative emotions in an audience by saturating them with scenes of brutality or death is a little off when the objectively descriptive language of vector analysis is used. Simply plunging an audience into a morass of brutality and death does not purge them of negative emotions. It is the full, direct impact of opposing sense vectors of equivalent magnitude that obliterates the negative emotions because nothing is left after a full impact and so a state of balance or harmony returns. For instance, a terrible sound can be eliminated by creating a direct impact with another sound wave of equivalent magnitude. Aristotle's ideas have never been abandoned because they were correct, if general, observations of what occurs with dramatic plots. Aristotle's observations correspond directly with vector theory.

The neoclassicists' notion of the Three Unities of Time, Place, and Action, on the other hand, fails to accurately define plot because it is a proscriptive theory, and narrowly so. Vector theory, like Aristotle's ideas, is descriptive, not proscriptive. Vector theory does not set limits on plot construction; it simply describes what occurs in plot construction. The neoclassical ideas were based on concepts of believability, and as such were value judgments. Since every culture in every period of history has considered its theater to be "real" (Clay, dissertation, 1956) the value judgments of what is real or believable are going to be as varied as the cultures are. One set of value judgments is not going to express all views of reality. To find what are universal principles behind plot construction, an objective description is necessary; an insistence on a proscriptive and culture-specific method of construction is useless.

Similarly, the notion of verisimilitude, comprised of the three goals of reality, morality, and generality, has again the problem of requiring the value judgments of one culture to define the elements of plot. Outside of the Western world, neither French neoclassical court culture nor the few fantastic and mythic subjects the neoclassicists deemed realistic—the Greek, Roman, and Bible myths— will have the meaning or even the believability they do to educated Westerners; therefore, the view of what is real to the neoclassicists is not universal. Further, views of morality and the understanding of truth are different to different societies and cultures, and so neoclassical proscriptions regarding morality and truth are also too limiting. A theory of plot based upon value judgments cannot be universal since such a theory is based on social and cultural bias.

The Delsarte System of acting was designed around the needs of the actors' instrument (body and voice), not on plotting. Nevertheless, it did address structure in that it identified typical forces in the portrayal of characters on the stages of the day: intellect (cognitions and abstractions), sentiment (emotions), and passion (physical drives). Intellect, sentiment, and passion as defined by Delsarte (and his society) are the underlying forces that affect the behavior of a character; this was the theory behind Delsarte's "scientific" charting of movement and vocal work. In a time where theatrical success was "star" driven, the interaction between a favorite leading lady expressing the force of sentiment and a favorite leading man expressing the force of intellect or passion was for Victorian audiences riveting because of the transformations that would occur in the characters. There was even a "star-vehicle" in the form of a play about Sherlock Holmes where Holmes was made to fall in love and marry—an astonishing transformation of Holmes, indeed. The Delsarte System worked for its audiences because it identified forces with which that society was concerned. As a system of creating characterization and dramatic excitement through character, the Delsarte System identified three different forces that affected human behavior and concerned itself with the interplay of those forces— the effects the forces have when converging, and the transformation of the characters as a result of that interplay. Although limited to characters as vehicles of forces, the Delsarte System nevertheless is consistent with vector theory and so the Delsarte System's continued impact on theater, dance, and music is not surprising.

For instance, I was part of a production of William Saroyan's *The Time of Your Life* in which the director insisted that when the villain entered the salon, the villain push the salon doors open with a gesture emanating from the villain's groin. It took some rehearsal time for the actor playing the villain to become used to the unfamiliar movement, but it soon became clear that the movement itself helped the actor to get into the character of a man driven only by "lower passions." Further, the simple gesture following Delsarte principles evoked each and every night of performance the reaction of recoiling, silencing distrust in the audience for the villain before the actor said one word of his lines. The gesture was an expression of the force of banal, dangerous emotions, and as such was readily perceived by the audience. In this case, although only one moment of the play was deliberately and consciously determined by Delsarte's System, the moment created the desired effect on the audience and was not in conflict with the otherwise Method thrust of the production.

As a theory that regards language, body language, and language of inflection (inflections impart meaningful communications in speech and song) (Werner, 1883, pg. xxviii) as being driven by "a phenomena of the soul" (Werner, pg. xxvi) and holds as a premise that there is a "*general law which controls the movements of the organs*" (Werner, p. 3 of Part I) the Delsarte System is based upon an intuitive understanding of what vector theory describes: the movements of bodies (organs) are controlled, determined by forces and the "form of each of these movements" can be understood and applied (Werner, p. 3 of Part I) to the actors' art.

The Well-Made Play Structure, the formula for writing plays invented by Eugene Scribe sets an index of pre-tested audience-pleasing events in the forms of exposition, misunderstandings, unexpected fortuitous or unfortuituous events, secrets, startling revelations, and sorting out of confusions in a causal relationship to each other to construct plots. The Well-Made Play Structure was never suggested as a universal theory of plot, merely a formula that well nigh guaranteed audience satisfaction. The Well-

Made Play Structure has been used continuously since its formation by Scribe, and is the scenario often underlying the worst and occasionally the best of plays. In the theater, why things work is important, but not nearly as important as the fact that they do. For this reason plus the fact that most plays built on the Well-Made Play Structure are awful clichéd pieces of tripe for all that they rake in the money, the principles behind this eminently successful formula have never been inquired into. However, going through the sequence of the Well-Made Play events for their causal relationship, it becomes clear that the logic of this formula follows vector theory quite tidily. First is the exposition; the exposition is defined in dramatic aesthetics as the opening establishment of who the key characters are, what the setting (the locale) is, what props (if any) are important, and what is going on—what the problem is. In other words, the exposition establishes the major vectors and what their senses are. Next in the Well-Made Play Structure some misunderstanding occurs. For instance, in *Babette's Feast*, a friend of the sisters urges them to take in a woman (Babette) who is a good cook to help them. The sisters do, and treat Babette as a housekeeper who is a good cook. This turns out to be a pivotal misunderstanding because Babette is not just a cook, she is a five-star chef. Here the misunderstanding arises from Babette's sense not being perceived because she has lost magnitude—she had to flee with only what she could carry from France and live in servitude in Denmark. Misunderstandings can be understood plot-wise as arising from a vector's direction, sense, or magnitude contrived to be imperfectly understood or not recognized by the other characters and/or the audience.

Next comes either a secret being kept or a fortuitous or unfortuitous event. In the case of *Babette's Feast*, a fortuitous event and a secret kept hidden occur simultaneously. Babette wins the lottery—an unexpected, fortuitous event. In the case of fortuitous events the protagonist converges with a positive sense vector which increases the protagonist's magnitude—Babette now has some financial power. In the case of unexpected unfortuitous event, the protagonist will converge with a negative sense vector which lessens (in the Well-Made Play Structure lessens greatly) the protagonist's magnitude. As for the secret, Babette chooses to keep her identity as stellar French chef a secret. The secret is representative of an important vector or a quality of an important vector. When the secret is maintained the vector is prevented from being added to the other same sense vectors and so the power of the vector cannot be fully realized. By maintaining her silence, the confusions about Babette continue to grow with the townspeople fearing she is a witch who will poison them with her meal. When the secret is at last revealed, typically as the startling revelation at the climax of a Well-Made Play, what is occurring is that all the vectors which affect the protagonist and the antagonist suddenly converge to transform the protagonist into a more powerful and more dimensional being than he or she had been believed to be. When it is revealed that Babette is a chef, it is also revealed that she spent all of her lottery winnings on the meal she created for the townspeople, her new friends. She is transformed from a penniless servant with some diabolical supernatural powers into an artist of the highest caliber who has the miraculous power of healing broken hearts through her generosity, sacrifice, and artistry.

The denouement of the Well-Made Play structure consists of the logical sorting out of the confusions. At the close of *Babette's Feast*, not only is Babette's true identity and value to her community now known, but the confusions of the characters of who they are and how they are to relate are resolved. When a few vectors remain to converge after the majority have at the climax, the resultants of these remaining forces' convergences are in keeping with that of the major convergence (the climactic convergence) ensuring the audience's sense of the structure's being finished. In The Well-Made Play

Structure, the sorting out of the confusions is the convergences of the vectors that did not converge with the majority at the climax. Thus, in *Babette's Feast*, just as the climax provided a happy resolution regarding Babette, so the little sortings out of the townspeople's problems created a denouement of small magnitude, positive resultants. The Well-Made Play Structure, seemingly a formula for ridiculously clichéd plays, is actually a sound enough formula of vector theory principles that it can and does provide a valid and reliable structure for stories of depth and dimension.

To continue considering the correspondences with vector theory with other dramatic aesthetic theories, *Yugen*, the aesthetic principle behind the Noh drama, refers to the quality of mystery and profundity that cannot be directly expressed in words (Tsunoda, De Bary, & Keene, 1958). The Noh actor, to be a master, is to imbue his performance with *Yugen*, to carry his performance beyond mere representation into the realm of transcendence. Noh actor and playwright Seami sought "to make of the Noh a symbolic theatre, in which the most important actions were not represented but suggested." (Tsunoda, et al. 1958). *Yugen* describes how the structure is to be expressed, not what structure the plot follows. *Yugen*, as the quality of mystery and profundity to be imbued in performances does suggest that an aspect of Noh Theater is concerned with a divine force that has mystery (positive sense) and profundity (great magnitude) as necessary qualities. Although *Yugen* could be regarded as a divine force influencing the performance, it is meant as the influence on the actor (as opposed to the character), on his dancing (as opposed to the dances), on the technique of playing the music, and on the build of the costumes, rather than the thematic forces the character with its dress, speech, and dance reveals about the story being told. *Yugen* is about the transcendental nature of art's essence; it is not about defining plot structure.

Returning to Occidental aesthetic theories and their

degree, if any, of correspondence to vector theory, the next well known theory is that of the tragic flaw. The theory of the tragic flaw, used most often to describe Shakespeare's plays and classical drama, holds that a character has one ruling quality which is the essence of his or her being and determines his or her destiny. This immutable quality propels him or her to act in certain ways at all times and so eventually brings the character to his or her doom. Thus, Brutus is driven to his doom by his sense of honor; Hamlet by his need to find the truth before he acts; and Macbeth by his ambition. The theory of the tragic flaw can be viewed as examining characters for their vector's direction and sense. Brutus has a direction of honor/dishonor and follows the positive sense of honor to his doom; Hamlet follows the direction of judgment with the positive sense of fairness, and so spends so much time in deliberation that he destroys his court; Macbeth follows the direction of ambition with the negative sense of greed to his doom. Though a very narrow form of analysis, the idea of the tragic flaw corresponds directly with vector analysis.

Antonin Artaud's dramatic aesthetic, Theater of Cruelty, was conceived by Artaud as a form of metaphysical catharsis and continues to be used by avant-garde theater productions as a theater of social revolt. Since Artaud conceived of Theater of Cruelty "as exceptional power of redirection" (Artaud, 1955, p. 83), Theater of Cruelty can be looked at as plotting used to disassemble the audience's point of view "as by a whirlwind of higher forces" (Artaud, p. 83), rather than assembling the audience's point of view. Vectorial analysis describes not only structures and construction, but it also describes destruction. Forces can be directed so that structures are destroyed in a specific and contained way, as those who work in the demolition of buildings with explosives can attest. Creating a script or performance that can be counted upon night after night to jolt audiences into freer awareness requires a very specific frame of mind. Needless to say there are few such scripts. *Le Roi de Maitre* is one, and Artaud himself called for Theater of Cruelty productions created from tales of the Marquis de Sade (Artaud, p. 99).

However, vector theory could greatly aid in the creation of new Theater of Cruelty plays. When characters, props, and settings are created to represent accepted social forces then it is easy enough to create other characters, props, and settings to represent forces of anarchy or other countering social ideals. The "sounds or noises that are unbearably piercing" (Artaud, p. 95); "light in waves, in sheets, in fusillades of fiery arrows" (Artaud, p. 95); "the hieroglyphic characters, ritual costumes, mannequins ten feet high representing the beard of King Lear in the storm, musical instruments tall as men, objects of unknown shape and purpose" (Artaud, p. 97-87), then become the anarchistic or rebellious forces having *directions* (course-ways) very different from the socially accepted forces—"man must resume his place between dream and events" (Artaud, p. 93), of *magnitudes* greater than the socially accepted forces—"mannequins ten feet high" and "musical instruments tall as men"; and *senses* that replace those of the socially accepted ones—"the beard of King Lear" [if we can fathom what *that* sense is]. The anarchistic forces basically would work to splice away separate, individual socially acceptable forces from the characters who are driven by many socially acceptable forces. Each individual socially acceptable force that is isolated then becomes easily obliterated by a direct impact with a more powerful anarchistic force.

The climax of the play would then be when the largest and last chunk of socially acceptable forces driving a character is obliterated; the character then would, as per vector theory, return to a natural state of balance, defined by Theater of Cruelty as being "between dream and events" (Artaud, p. 93). For this reason, a man suddenly strapped to a chair by men in white lab coats, then left alone in terror, only to have a huge chicken run out and circle him squawking shrilly and running away again, as I have seen in a Theater of Cruelty performance, is dramatically satisfying while being at the same time a bizarre jolt. Theater of Cruelty tends to be used during times of social upheaval as a means of creating the upheaval, and is successful in this because it follows the principles of vector theory. Vector theory describes destruction and torsion as precisely as it does construction and stability.

Vector theory is perhaps the most analogous with the dramatic aesthetic Theory of Conflict; conflict theory being in effect a simplistic and violence emphasized version of vector theory. Conflict theory, the currently prevailing theory of plot, has created enormous problems in literature and drama. What these problems are and why they plague the literary and dramatic works built on conflict theory is the subject of the next chapter. Here, though, the correspondences between conflict theory and vector theory will be examined.

Conflict theory holds that it is the oppositional *relationship* between the characters that is important, rather than who the characters are or what they do; thus, conflict theory presumes drama and literature to be a dynamic— an interactive system involving conflicting forces. Conflict theory moves away from the approaches of Delsarte and Stanislavsky which center on characterization as effecting plot, and approaches plot as being effected by the *interactions* of the opposing forces. Conflict theory defines the nature of this interaction as oppositional, confrontational, antagonistic, even violent.

Defining plot as the oppositional interaction (conflict) between characters is a huge shift in conceptualization. From this understanding of conflict theory, two things become apparent at once: one, that a major problem with conflict theory is that characterization is no longer central and so is easily glossed over; and two, that conflict theory is most clearly related in its language as defining a dynamic, and the study and language of dynamics is vector theory based. By shifting the emphasis from the characters to the dynamic of their oppositional interaction, conflict theory moves from the description of the characters and the forces they embody to a description of the nature of the interactions between the characters as a result of the converging of the forces. This was a great contribution to literary and dramatic aesthetics because it clarifies the distinction and the relation between characterization and plot, defines the nature of plot (if incorrectly as fighting), and more definitely defines the climax (instead of "the most exciting moment coming at the end") as the greatest, final, and determining moment of struggle between the opposing forces (also incorrect).

Basically, in Conflict, each succeeding moment of struggle between the characters exceeds the previous ones until a final struggle determines who is the victor or if all fail (failure usually taking the form of death). The denouement usually consists of moments expressing exultation if the protagonist has won, despair and grief if the villain has won, and shock or relief if they both have lost. This simplistic form corresponds directly with vector theory: Each struggle is greater because the character-vectors have acquired more magnitude and/or because their impacts are increasingly more direct. The final struggle is climactic because it is clearly final: one of the two sets of forces is of such magnitude as to sustain the nearly direct or completely direct impact while the other set of forces are nearly or completely obliterated, and the full, or nearly full impact creates a markedly new force. Thus, conflict theory is an expression of vector theory in its most rude form.

There are notable omissions and some severe errors in conflict theory. Conflict theory tends to mark only the moments of struggle (destructive convergences, with one or more of the vectors loosing magnitude) as important, not the moments when magnitude is gained. The concept of opposition is regarded as conflicting forces only, never as countering forces; and the climax is too narrowly defined as the result of a fight. These errors arise from implicit value judgments that aggression is exciting, problems are only solved through destruction of opposing points of view, and that happiness is created by the person "in the right" getting his way. In essence then, while conflict theory has been the aesthetic theory that has hither-to most clearly and most accurately defined plot, its notions are reflections of certain cultural biases that limit its universality.

Conflict theory has worked so well because it is such an accurate if simplistic form of vector theory principles. Interestingly, Hegel's original notion of "tragic conflict" was that "the action [of drama] is driven forward by the unstable equilibrium between man's will and his environment—the wills of other men, the forces of society and of nature" (Lawson, 1960, p. 37). Hegel "observed that certain laws of motion are inherent in the movement of things; and that the same laws of motion govern the processes of the mind" (Lawson, p. 35). The laws of motions are described in dynamics by vector analysis, and Hegel's use of the word conflict clearly refers to the idea of dynamics, not of supremacy. Hegel's concept of "tragic conflict" as imbalance in dynamics was altered to become today's version of the struggle of man's will to dominate by Ferdinand Brunetiere who was "deeply conservative; his philosophy tended toward fideism" (Lawson, p. 59). (Fideism is to rely on faith rather than scientific reasoning.) Brunetiere held that "drama lies in man's attempt to dominate his surroundings" and so came to redefine Hegel's "tragic conflict" as the "law of conflict." "The drama is the representation of the will of man in conflict with the mysterious powers or natural forces which limit and belittle us...struggle against fatality, against social law, against one of his fellow mortals, against himself... against...the malevolence of those who surround him" (Lawson, p. 59). Even in Brunetiere's redefinition of conflict theory, Conflict is not so narrowly defined as it tends to be today. In contemporary thinking, Conflict is often seen as limited to a conflict between two characters or two groups of characters, not of abstractions like fatality.

Aside from Hegel's tragic conflict which has devolved into today's conflict theory, one of the most radical and important changes in dramatic aesthetics is The Method. Although The Method is chiefly concerned with characterization both in who the character is and how the character effects plot, the specifics of the theory are also directly analogous to vector theory. The main thrust for action to occur in a play or story from The Method perspective is that each character has an objective that is actively pursued. That is, the events of the production are created by the characters as a means towards a result of following goals. The climax is understood to be the moment when the main characters either accomplish their objectives or fail. "Following the objective" as The Method actors say, implies the character is following a trajectory that is intended to arrive in a specific, transforming resultant, and this understanding is important artistically to the actor. As the protagonist follows his or her objective, the tactics followed are changed as result of meetings with characters of similar and dissimilar objectives. The moment of these changes, called "beat changes" are considered dramatically key moments of the production with the more profound beat changes being the more dramatically significant. Accomplishment of aspects of the objectives and what the results of such accomplishments are create the most dramatic moments. Therefore, inherent in The Method's form of analysis is the concept of different characters, locales, and even props being transformed as a result of their meeting and interacting with each other. This assumed truism of The Method can be more precisely described through vector analysis which clarifies that it is the forces governing the characters, locales, and props that propel them towards convergences and change the characters, locales, and props by transforming the forces that move them into new forces during the rising action, and transforming these forces into a single, new force at the climax with a resultant change in the characters, locals, and props themselves.

Method analysis of the script for character objectives and for the beat changes, particularly the beat changes, is a lengthy process with the precise beat changes occasionally not being finally determined upon until quite late in the rehearsal process or even during the run of the show. This occurs because the decisions about when a beat change occurs or even what is a beat change in a given scene sometimes has been left to a trial and error process as no exacting, objective, reliable definition of the elements of plot has been available to indicate what the moments of transformation are and what the transformation is. Vector theory will alleviate if not eliminate this problem. What happens when, where, and why can all be described precisely by vector theory, and since the process of following objectives to accomplishment and transformation can be precisely understood the process can be followed more exactly. The better a process is understood the easier it is to render it artistically. Thus vector theory can facilitate Method analysis.

Metaphorical analysis, being the form of analysis imperative to directors and designers, is concerned with creating the artistic piece in its totality, the full and complete structure, and does this by identifying the key elements of a dramatic work and by determining at exactly what moments those elements transform. Clearly, this process is analogous to identifying forces and determining when and where those forces converge to create new forces. In metaphorical analysis, the elements and their moments of transformation are developed into aspects of a central metaphorical image (an emotive symbol) to give them organic cohesiveness with each other. Just as in vector analysis different bodies are regarded as being driven by the countering or opposing forces, in metaphorical analysis different elements of a dramatic work (the characters, props, and sets) are depicted as different symbols which graphically illustrate the true nature of the dramatic work's elements; in other words, symbols are chosen to show what forces the characters, props, or sets are moved by. The metaphorical image, or production concept, is chosen to suggest the ultimate change that is going to occur in the play, for an ultimate change, or a transformation, is assumed to occur at the climax of every production which is a work of art. This axiom that the climax is a moment of transformation corresponds directly with the notion in vector analysis that the convergence of forces creates a resultant new force. The segregating of the elements of a play into different symbols and then relating those separate symbols in such a way as to create equivalence between their relationship and another single symbol corresponds to the mathematical principle of creating functions and equations. An equation is the relating of a variable or constant as equivalent to a relationship between other variables, or other variables and constants. (A variable is a quantity that can assume any of a set of values and a constant is a quantity assumed to have a fixed value).

When the constant or variable that is related as equivalent to the relationship of the other variables and/or constants is then used within another equation as part of quantities that relate in such a way as to be equivalent to yet another quantity, then that constant or variable is said to be a function of the equation creating the new quantity. Thus, if a character is said to be sly, clever, and dangerous and then the character is symbolized as a fox in his costuming and mannerisms, the symbol of the fox is understood by Occidental cultures to be equivalent to the relationship between slyness, cleverness, and dangerousness. The fox symbol, then, becomes a function within a production concept wherein other functions of characters such as a witch, a little piggy, mean elves, a bunny, and a mighty hunter, etc. relate to let the audience know the play being performed is the same as a classical children's fairy tale. This is the case in the TV film *A

Christmas Story. Ralphie, the main character fights with a boy costumed to suggest a fox; Ralphie's little brother is called "Mama's little piggy" and costumed in a snow suit to resemble a little pig; Ralphie's teacher is depicted as a witch when she gives him a less-than-hoped-for grade; he encounters mean looking elves on the way to Santa; he receives a bunny outfit his mother makes him put on; and he dreams of owning a Red Rider BB gun resembling a hunter's rifle. All aspects of the television film are skillfully and subtly reflective of the production concept that *A Christmas Story* is a classic children's fairy tale. The function of depicting a character as a fox, a little piggy, or a witch is to demonstrate that all the functions together (fox, piggy, witch, etc) are equivalent to the single symbol of the production concept—in this case, a classic children's fairy tale. The relationship between a character who is sly, clever, and dangerous could not be understood as the symbol of a fox unless the fox is emotionally understood as a force that has the direction of slyness (appears and disappears furtively), the magnitude of cleverness, and the negative sense of posing a danger. Because the symbol represents not just the character but a force everyone has experienced the effects of, identifying the character with the symbol makes the qualities of the character more profoundly emotionally affecting to the audience. Thus, vector theory clarifies why a metaphorical analysis and the creation of a metaphorical image is vital to creating a true work of dramatic art.

Aristotle tried to define the universal elements and workings of plot structure but was only able to name parts of the plot without defining them precisely. More than a millennium later, the neoclassicists endeavored to create a definition of plot based upon Aristotle's ideas but cast in the light of their value judgments of believability. More centuries passed, until Scribe unabashedly devised a sound formula for constructing plots to make himself rich and Delsarte formulated a philosophy of acting which holds as a premise that there is a general, scientific, law or principle which controls all movement that can be understood and applied to the human languages of movement, inflection, and words. Another century passed and a proliferation of dramatic aesthetic notions arise: the concept of the tragic flaw which picks out one quality of a character as the key element that drives the character's behavior and so the plot; Artaud's Theater of Cruelty which is to jolt, jar, and shock out of audiences ossified social views for the audience members' greater well-being; Stanislavsky's Method which seeks to define when, how, and why characters change what they do and who they are; conflict theory which establishes that it is the dynamic between the characters that shapes the plot; and metaphorical analysis which seeks to unify and shape theatrical productions through the creation of an embracing and transcending metaphorical image. With the one exception of the neoclassicists' notions, each of these aesthetic theories of the theater shares basic conceptualizations with vector theory.

Aristotle identified the basic structure of dramatic plot: rising action, climax, falling action. Aristotle's determination that drama has structure which can be generally plotted is directly analogous with vector analysis which is used to plot structures. Scribe worked out a formula that would guarantee a play would have rising action that was exciting to the audience, a climax that was satisfyingly startling and transforming, and a falling action that related properly to the climax. Scribe's formula is as successful as good mathematical formulas are; one plugs in certain elements in the right places in relation to each other and the wanted result is created. Scribe's formula corresponds directly with vector theory principles in the formulation that certain sorts of convergences are needed to direct forces to become "concurrent" — forming a unified structure. Delsarte hypothesized the existence of a scientifically applicable law governing movement which would impel human languages of motion, inflection, and word to behave in certain, chartable ways. Although he is not recorded as precisely defining that scientific law governing movement, mathematicians have done so with vector theory. Engineers have defined for inanimate objects what Delsarte claimed happens to human expression; forces (what Delsarte understood as "phenomena of the spirit") act in characteristic manners and affect bodies accordingly.

Antonin Artaud was concerned with returning the human mind to its ability to work in a transcendent, metaphysical manner by breaking it from everyday reality into the reality of dreams through a controlled and directed process of destruction of experiential norms. Similarly, vector theory is used in engineering to destroy structures or bodies in a controlled and directed manner. The Method is concerned with what is happening—who is behaving how— moment by moment and at what moments significant changes in behavior or being occur. Vector analysis also is concerned with the same questions charting graphically the movements of forces, their magnitude, direction, and their sense (way of behaving) and indicating those points where the action lines of forces meet resulting in the new directions and magnitudes of the forces or the creation of utterly new forces.

Conflict theory is concerned with the dynamic relations between the elements, and so corresponds directly with vector theory in the notion that it is the result of the countering elements acting upon each other that plots the structure. Metaphorical analysis is also directly analogous with vector analysis in that the characters, props, and settings of drama are regarded as being driven by thematic forces. Metaphorical analysis considers that the characters, props, and settings can be best understood when they are visually represented as grouped according to the kind of thematic force to which they belong. The dramatic piece is considered to occur within a temporal "playing space" which is best expressed by a specific metaphorical image—a production concept—that sums up the actions of the different thematic forces. When each of these traditional dramatic aesthetics is paired with the conceptualizations of vector theory their importance and usefulness becomes even clearer and the facility with which they may be utilized increases. Vector theory enhances traditional forms of dramatic analysis because it provides a systematic means to separate out the differing forces so that the forces may then be identified and symbolized through the traditional forms of dramatic analysis.

Chapter Seven
Vector Theory, Conflict Theory, and Feminist Theory

The theory of conflict, or Conflict, is the currently prevailing theory of plot construction. Conflict theory has such a hold on literary and dramatic analysis that it is not unusual to find plot defined as "the conflict (plot) involving protagonist and antagonist" (Guerin, Labor, Morgan, Reesman, & Willingham, 1992, p. 9) and defined again as "plot structure, the relatedness of actions, the gradual buildup in suspense from a situation full of potential to a climax and a resolution." (Guerin, et al, 1992, p. 11) This second definition, while useful, still has the difficulty of no precise definition of the word "climax." For many literary people and theatrical artists, the buildup of suspense is regarded as having been created out of the conflict between the protagonist and the antagonist. The theory of conflict is problematic because it limits artistry, causes the misinterpretation of some literary and dramatic works, and promotes the creation of ethically troubling literary and dramatic pieces. Basically, conflict theory is an oversimplification of vector theory and it is this oversimplification which has led to a variety of creative and ethical problems.

Conflict theory whittles down the quantity of vectors to their smallest number, creating

limited interest matter; and the notion of Conflict confuses the concept of forces countering each other with violence.

This is obvious in the usual Hollywood offerings of films where the bad guys are forces of evil (negative vectors) and have the objective (direction) of controlling the world (nation, state, city, or woman) while the good guys are forces of good (positive vectors) and have the objective (direction) of controlling the world (nation, state, city, or woman). The final show-down between the two vectors (bad guys as evil force and good guys as good force) takes place at the coveted seat of power at a specified time (with the show-down being more of a shoot-up), and the champion (the biggest of the bad guys or the biggest of the good guys) of the more powerful vector emerges mutilated but triumphant. That this hackneyed formula is usually successful in creating tightly structured films with dramatic climaxes is not due merely to two strong men making each other bleed (conflict) but to the fact that the formula follows vector theory with stringent, if narrow, precision. The antagonist and the protagonist meet (converge) at the same time in the same place and a positive (if the protagonist wins the battle) or negative (if the antagonist wins the battle) resultant is produced.

Conflict theory asks who is in opposition to whom. This is very much in keeping with vector theory in that a structure is created through opposing forces. However, even on this very basic level there are problems with Conflict. One is that it is frequently assumed that two *people* are in opposition to each other when there are extant a vast number of literary and dramatic works where things are in opposition with themselves or other things. For example, science fiction works tend to have asteroids or other inert bodies on a collision course with the planet earth. Conflict theory has been taken to mean only characters are in opposition to each other, which neglects the importance of other aspects of literary and dramatic pieces such as location or objects.

For instance, in E. M. Forester's novel *Howard's End*, the locale, the countryside house Howard's End works as a vector. The force of the countryside house causes the characters to act according to their true promptings, recognize who they are, and face their pasts. Helen and Paul act upon their attraction for each other by kissing under the tree, but they recognize he is not free to pursue Helen. Facing that their kissing has initiated a chain of events which could lead to marriage they hastily work to prevent that outcome, and all of this introduces the main character, Meg, to Mrs. Wilcox, who is part of the vector set of Howard's End. Charles Wilcox, the elder son, also acts too aggressively—his actions result in the death of Leonard. That all these revelations take place at Howard's End indicates that that countryside house indeed represents a vector of great magnitude (the ability to draw people to and away from it), with a clear-cut direction (the path between confusion and self-knowledge as symbolized by coming towards or going away from Howard's End), and with a positive sense (the self-awareness it causes in others). This problem with Conflict being considered as only occurring between characters is in actuality an error some film artists and theater artists make through ignorance of Ferdinand Brunetiere's law of conflict which clearly states the struggles depicted in drama may occur "'against fatality, against social law, against one of his own fellow mortals, against himself'" (Lawson, 1960 p. 59).

Underlying this error of seeing Conflict as only occurring between characters is the misunderstanding that it is the bodies—characters, objects, or locales—that are set in opposition to each other when a better description of what is occurring is that it is the forces affecting the bodies that are in opposition. A rock is just a rock, but where and how the forces drive that rock is all important, whether it be an uncaring, capricious universe hurtling an asteroid at the earth, or the force of anger that urges a man to hurl a rock at his neighbors. It is important to distinguish between forces and bodies. Forces act upon bodies to create predictable responses or movement or stasis in the bodies. Bodies in the form of characters do not activate themselves.

In The Method, stage movement (blocking and business) are said to be created out of "internal promptings" or "urges" which are developed through the subtext (the thoughts and feelings the character has but does not speak of out loud). In The Method it is assumed that a character does not cross the stage for no reason; there is something (the force of a thought or feeling) that propels the character to act. Clearly objects and locations will do nothing unless they are imbued with some sort of power that allows them to affect characters and other things. When bodies are confused with the forces that move them then incorrect interpretations are made of dramatic pieces and fiction.

I once listened to the frustration of a playwright whose play was being misinterpreted by the director. The director was making the common error that so many practitioners of conflict theory make: he was assuming the conflict was between two specific characters since he was trained to find an antagonist in the form of one character, and a protagonist in the form of another character. The playwright felt that the conflict was between Time and the characters, not between the characters. In the theater, the director makes the final decision and so the playwright's view was not what was expressed in the production of the play. The result was that a script of great pathos was marred by an incorrect interpretation that sought to force a conflict between characters when those characters actually belonged to the same vector. The main characters argued loudly and stridently during dialogue that was actually about their anguish over their opposition to Time. The playwright, knowing her script's meaning, understood that the vectors were mortality and Time, not the two individual characters. The confusing of the forces with the bodies hurt the production although fine acting undid much of the bad directing.

The concept of some sort of impetus, force, propelling the bodies (characters, props, and locales) of literature and drama is as important to aesthetic theory as it is to mathematical theory. For aesthetics, it is the identity and statement of underlying forces that give a literary or dramatic piece its transcendent meaning. In the case of the director's interpretation of the play versus the playwright's, the director's narrow focus on conflict theory caused him to miss the play's transcendent meaning.

Another problem of Conflict's question of who is in opposition to whom, is the insistence that the vectors be limited to only two—two vectors in opposition to each other. Here again, this belies the many literary and dramatic works that have subplots; a piece with subplots has by definition more than one set of vectors. By defining plot as a single conflict between a protagonist and an antagonist, the scope of literary and dramatic art is curtailed. By suggesting that plot is constructed out of only two opposing vectors—the conflict between the antagonist and the protagonist—conflict theory does not accurately describe vast numbers of literary and dramatic works. *King Lear* would not be the masterpiece it is without its subplots. *King Lear* will be discussed in more detail later in this chapter.

Perhaps the most ethically problematic aspect of Conflict is the underlying concept that the opposition between the protagonist and the antagonist is an antagonism between foes. This problem originates with Brunetiere who altered Hegel's view of tragic conflict as "the unstable equilibrium between man's will and his environment." (Lawson, 1960, p. 37) Naturally a concept of antagonism leads to the creation of works of literature and drama that emphasize and showcase violence. Conflict is normally defined as a struggle or fight, and so is often equated with violence, especially violence at the climax. This is faulty for various reasons. A salient reason is that violence only creates the desire for more extreme violence (August Staub, classroom lecture, Oct., 1982) rather than bringing on a feeling of resolution. Violence is not transformative. Ironically, violence can be considered antithetical to aesthetics because aesthetics is about the transformation of emotions, ways of being, and meanings into new emotions, new ways of being, and new meanings while violence only evokes in readers and audiences a taste for more and more violence. As violence is considered to be the natural result of conflict, the sheer number of works showcasing violence becomes in itself an ethical problem.

More interesting films, like *Lorenzo's Oil*, make use of a greater array of vectors—ravages of disease countered by parental sacrifice, intellectual obtuseness countered by logical inquiry, ignorance countered by knowledge, racism countered by friendship, misunderstanding countered by forgiveness, the morality of the acceptance of death countered by love's imperative. Thus, vectors may be myriad in number and may converge in a resultant of intellectual and emotional exultation rather than the simplistic convergence of a mere two vectors in a revolting resultant of petty triumph. Violence need not ever enter a work for the work to sustain interest and culminate in a highly exciting climax.

Furthermore, the equation of violence with conflict leads to the notion that any climax that is not violent is therefore not climactic, e.g.: dull, boring, a "let-down." The notion that a climax is exciting only if it is violent is a false assertion. The Broadway musical *The Secret Garden* demonstrates that a climax need not be violent to be exciting. Indeed, the climax of this show is based on violence's opposite—empathy, compassion, and love. The climactic moment of this musical is when the father of the sickly boy tells the boy's uncle (the father's brother) that the uncle has spent so many years looking after father and child that the uncle has a right to go and live his own life.

This is an amazing moment because even though the uncle has deviously sought to keep the boy sickly (if not kill him), throw the boy's orphaned cousin out, and to take over the estate, the father successfully and easily ends the uncle's machinations through love and kindness, not violence. The excitement comes from the various vectors represented by the children and the father converging, causing the children and father to come into full power at the same time the uncle must be confronted. The antagonistic vectors represented by the uncle and the protagonistic forces represented by the children and father have come together tightly at the same time and at the same place. Further, the magnitudes of each of the positive vectors represented by the orphaned girl, the sickly boy, the bereaved father—seem weak, and yet when they are joined together at their convergence their union magnifies their power and shows just how strong the vectors propelling these characters truly are. The sudden revelation of great magnitude is startling but entirely plausible. Not only is violence not needed at the climactic convergence, it would be out of place. The climax of *The Secret Garden* is thrilling. Too often has the equation of violence with conflict led to a failure to create truly thrilling moments within literary and dramatic works.

Conflict theory, in modern usage, has become about the tension of opposition, and this leads to yet more problems. The emphasis on opposites causes writers and playwrights to restrict themselves to the smallest number of vectors—usually a mere pair. Although this is helpful in that it simplifies the creative process, it is detrimental in that it leads to simplistic creations. Works with only one set of countering forces are going to be one-dimensional—which so many works that feature a "bad" guy and a "good" guy are. Such films, like the many cowboy and Indian films of the fifties and early sixties, are notorious for their simplistic structure and the mindless prejudice of their messages. Regarding the countering forces as antagonistic foes, and assigning the moral judgment of "bad" to the negative vector and "good" to the positive vector with the positive vector representing a favored population (regardless of the facts of history) has contributed more to creating social ills than to creating art. Oversimplification in the form of describing an entire people as a single negative force to be destroyed by a different people that is a single force of good is both artistically poor and ethically wrong. Nevertheless, such over-simplifications are a hallmark of works using Conflict as the guiding theory for plot construction.

Another way in which Conflict oversimplifies the creative process is that Conflict is often described as the tension between two separate characters, thus often losing sight of the fact one character may be driven by different vectors and so have both positive and negative senses. In "The Tell-Tale Heart" by Edgar Allen Poe, the central character, who narrates the story, is affected by different vectors and so vacillates between senses. At times he is motivated by feelings of love: "I loved the old man" (positive vector), and at other times by fear and dread (negative vector). "He had the eye of a vulture—a pale blue eye, with a film over it. Whenever it fell upon me, my blood ran cold; and so by degrees—very gradually—I made up my mind to take the life of the old man..." The central character's direction is the path between sanity and insanity: "How, then, am I mad? Hearken! And observe how healthily—how calmly I can tell you the whole story." There is conflict in "The Tell Tale Heart," but it arises not from two separate characters in conflict, but from one character who has warring vectors within himself. The horror of the story arises from the fact that the old man is an innocent victim of a war of forces in another person. Conflict theory tends towards stories where the antagonist is one character and the protagonist is another instead of stories such as Poe's where the countering forces exist in one character only.

Yet another way in which Conflict oversimplifies composition is that its approach is formulaic. In one common formula, the protagonist and antagonist have the same direction; for instance, both may want to rule the world. In formulas characters become mere types rather than individuals. Lost to formula are plots where many directions are explored through the focus on different vectors; lost to formula are plots where the protagonist or the antagonist tries new strategies for fulfilling their motivations by following the course (direction) of a different vector that is nevertheless of the same sense as the other vectors that have driven them. Nor, in formulaic works, do character vectors' directions coincide and then separate, (due a convergence of their same-sense vectors) combining the characters' efforts for a time.

The novel *Jane Eyre* demonstrates how the splitting off of vectors through convergences reveals different vectorial direction and brings enrichment to a piece. Jane Eyre and her Mr. Rochester have as a shared direction romance. They head along this path the same way—towards marriage. However, at the point when they should be married they are separated through a startling revelation. Their directions have each changed because a convergence with other vectors forces them to ally themselves with different vectors. Mr. Rochester must ally himself with lawful duty by suffering his marriage to his insane wife. Jane must ally herself with the vector of Christian virtue. Thus, Mr. Rochester returns to his manor and wife. Jane departs and becomes part of a household of a would-be Christian missionary. Mr. Rochester is realigned with lawful duty, Jane with Christianity.

Jane's flight is an effort to maintain her privilege to enter heaven (heaven-seeking vector), but it totally impoverishes her. Her aunt, who has always been her antagonist, finds herself with the need to earn the privilege of entering heaven (heaven-seeking vector). Thus, Jane and the aunt converge as weak vectors (heaven-seeking and Christian virtue vectors) joining a larger vector, a more surely heaven-bound vector. The aunt's direction has changed because her desire for heaven (heaven-seeking vector) is stronger than her negative vector of sin, when the sin vector and the heaven-seeking vector converge at the moment of mortal illness. As Jane has followed a course (direction) of Christian virtue, she and the aunt converge as same-sense vectors as they both hope to attain heaven (heaven-bound vector). The aunt retracted a lie she had told an uncle of Jane's, the lie being that Jane was dead; the lie was originally made to prevent the uncle from bequeathing Jane his money. The heaven-bound vector overcomes the sin vector when they converge. As the vector of greater magnitude, the heaven-bound vector has a powerful resultant—Jane gains an earthly triumph in the receipt of money, and the aunt triumphs, for she will be more likely to go to heaven because a retraction of her lie (the destruction of the sin vector) helps to cleanse her soul (removes that particular sin vector from her). As two vectors both traveling towards heaven, Jane and the aunt both triumph through their convergence: two same sense vectors, being added together through convergence gain in magnitude and have their directions (course-ways) shifted that much more accurately towards heaven.

There is yet another set of vectors that reveal themselves through the focus of direction—sex. The missionary becomes enamored of Jane and wishes to marry her. His desire constitutes a negative vector because if Jane marries him and goes with him as a missionary she will die in the tropical setting very quickly, and that does not seem to bother the missionary. Since Jane offers to go as his secretary, not his wife, the missionary tells her that would classify her as a loose woman, "for when just now I repeated the offer of serving him for a deacon, he expressed himself shocked at my want of decency. He seemed to think I had committed an impropriety in proposing to accompany him unmarried." The missionary's motivations are thusly established as questionable: he is moved by a negative vector—lust. The missionary wants Jane in the wifely role of bedfellow more than as a fellow in Christ. Jane is tempted to go. The missionary is very handsome and compelling. Jane has the choice of experiencing her sexuality in the short-lived, heady world of tropical delight far from her natural home (negative vector of lust), or she can experience it in the more temperate manner of motherhood in her native land (positive vector of marital "duty"). In this case Jane rejects the offer of missionary ecstasy and sexual ecstasy in favor of the choice, represented by Rochester, of simple, dutiful, daily joy. Jane chooses the ugly man (Rochester) over the handsome one (the missionary). Aligning herself with the vector of earthly joys instead of that of Christian proselytizing and lust, the depth of meaning of the novel is further revealed by the exploration of the various directions the different vectors have. This is just a sampling of the richness that the concept of the vectorial quality of direction brings to Charlotte Bronte's novel. The theory of conflict stumbles in pieces like *Jane Eyre* because it would try to define the missionary solely either in the negative sense as seducer or in the positive sense of a savior of souls.

Another problem is that Conflict rarely makes a distinction between the separate elements of sense and direction. Often, when no distinction is made between sense and direction no true motivation is given to a character. The protagonist is "good" just because he is, and the antagonist is "bad" just because he is. That a distinction between sense and direction is important is evident in *King Lear*. Lear's direction is that of sovereign power. His sense is positive because he wishes to bestow power and is motivated by his love for and generosity towards his daughters. The direction of sovereign power is different from what is done with the power. Direction and sense are also differentiated in Goneril and Regan. They also move along the path of power. Their sense is negative—they wish to take power and are motivated by greed and power-lust. Since they have duly been chosen for a life of power by birth and by Lear's bequest to them, power is the path in life they have been given. However, they seek further power through deception, betrayal, murder, and war. Lear and his two elder daughters have the same direction—power—but different senses. The motivations of love and generosity and greed and power-lust are antithetical senses. A differentiation between sense and direction is also evident in Cordelia's character. Her objective is to speak the truth; her direction is the path between silence and speech. (Her refusal at first to tell Lear how much she loves him hurts him, but later her words revive him on his sick bed.) Cordelia is motivated by love. "Unhappy that I am, I cannot heave my heart into my mouth." Her heart is full of love, but since she cannot speak of it, she opts for speaking the truth.

Lear and Cordelia have the same sense, but different directions as they are governed by different vectors. When they converge at the forgiveness scene (IV, vii), they unite into the same vector (Lear's of sovereign power), and though their magnitude increases, it is not enough to be triumphant. Cordelia is too young and Lear is too old and so their magnitude is too weak even when combined. Goneril and Regan are very strong when united because they have the same sense and direction and individually have much magnitude. During the course of the play, Goneril and Regan set themselves up in opposition to each other through the force of jealousy; they both take Edmund as a lover and this divides them. When Goneril and Regan converge again as opposing forces, they destroy each other because vectors of equivalent magnitude that impact completely annihilate each other. Lear and his daughters are all destroyed, and so the original state of the kingdom is reestablished. At the beginning of the play the kingdom is united under one king. At the end of the play the kingdom is united under one king—the good son of Gloucester, Edgar. While the destruction of all the vector characters of the main plot of *King Lear* means the original state is re-established, the subplot of *King Lear*, the story of Edgar's trials and tribulations, is constructed to make Edgar triumphant over all the vectors that opposed him. Thus, Edgar becomes, is transformed into, the vector that Lear originally was--the sovereign of England.

Originally Edgar was the positive sense quality of the vector that had the direction of filial duty. When Edgar is transformed by the climactic convergence, his sense remains positive, but he becomes the vector that has the direction of sovereign power. His sense stays the same but his direction changes because he becomes transformed into the focus of a new vector. Cordelia and Lear had the same sense, positive, but were of different vectors until they united at the reconciliation scene and Cordelia becomes part of the sovereign power vector Lear embodies. Goneril and Regan have the same direction as Lear, but negative sense. The differentiation of sense and direction give much of the richness to Shakespeare's relentlessly tragic script.

Lack of distinction between sense and direction also leads conflict theory to minimalize the falling action. In works constructed through the theory of conflict, one common problem is that the triumph of the more powerful vector tends to be unquestionably good or bad and so is easily forgotten. This happens when the sense of each major vector is reduced to a nebulous form. The protagonist is motivated by Good, the antagonist by Evil. Identification with the sense of either vector is superficial, and so the resultant of the convergence has no real consequence. Further, little transformation may occur because there is little change in the triumphant vector's direction. If the hero is triumphant, the audience or reader knows he will continue to want to right wrongs. If the villain is triumphant, the audience or reader knows he will continue to try to wreak havoc. This is fine for light entertainment but it readily grows stale. Those readers or audiences looking for a transformative experience will not receive it because there is no character who has been transformed. Super Man remains Super Man, ever unchanging.

The last and perhaps greatest deficiency of conflict theory is that conflict does not exist in all plays and tales.

Some works are more concerned with a careful structuring of theme than they are of storyline. In these pieces characters are not so much representations of individuals as they are of intangibles—ideals, feelings, aspects of human understanding, or elements of the divine. In such symbolic works, where events are important more because of what they mean than because they cause other events, plot is still comprised of forces which must converge and transform. Hence, in Maurice Materlink's "The Intruder," there are three different sorts of vectors, none of which are meant to depict people: vectors of universal emotion (denial as personified by the uncle; fear and foreboding as personified by the grandfather; suffering as characterized by the wife; and helplessness as characterized by the infant), vectors of the supernatural (the approach of death as evidenced by the silence of the birds, the sound of the scythe and the footsteps, and the grandfather's prescience of these events), and vectors of archetypal imagery. The nineteenth century belief that there was an ancient three-fold goddess (Hutton, p. 36, 2000) is given archetypal form in the play by two elements: the three daughters representing the maiden form of the goddess, and the Sister of Mercy representing the goddess in destructive form. These three different sorts of vectors— emotion, the supernatural, and archetypal images—converge at the moment of Death's arrival and create a negative resultant of pathos and horror. The resultant is a negative one because the majority of the vectors are negative—feelings of fear, the approach of Death, and the presence of the archetype of the destructive form of the goddess in the guise of the Sister of Mercy. Thus, the play ends with the grandfather (an archetypal image of both a Wise Old Man and a Hero) is forced to face what he dreads most—being left alone in his blindness in the company of Death—a powerful and chilling resultant, indeed.

Maeterlink's "The Intruder" shows how the theory of vectors better describes the workings of Symbolist works' plots than does the currently prevailing theory of conflict. There is no real conflict in "The Intruder." In the opening of the play Death is coming, in middle of the play Death is coming, and in the end Death arrives. Some of the characters are aware of Death's coming and fear it; other characters have no idea Death is approaching. None of the characters fights Death's approach; none of the characters tries to prevent Death from arriving.

John Synge's "Riders to the Sea" presents the same situation; conflict is not to be had. The play opens with the mother insisting her missing son has drowned at sea; the middle of the play consists of the last living son asserting that he, too, will go out to the sea despite the forebodings of his death the mother has; and the play ends with the last son's drowned corpse being carried on stage. "Riders to the Sea" cannot be easily analyzed in terms of conflict, and yet without a doubt the play has a climactic and powerful finish. Once understood as a group of converging vectors the structure of the piece is readily discerned. Together the characters are of the force of human effort and will, and individually they belong to other forces. The character-vector of the mother is a force of despair and foreboding; the daughters are of a force of innocence and fear; the son of a vector of perseverance; and the sea is the symbol of the relentless forces of death and nature. The climactic moment of the play, the point where these vectors converge in the same time and place, the carrying in of the sea-drenched, drowned last son, produces a negative resultant—no human force can stand against the tide of death. The play ends on a note of doom and grief. Vector theory, unlike conflict theory, provides for a meaningful analysis of the structure of "The Riders to the Sea" and "The Intruder" because it allows for each of the plays' components to be analyzed instead of forcing the focus of study to just two warring characters.

Conflict theory, then, is fallacious for three overriding reasons. First, it is such an oversimplified description of the workings of fiction that it encourages the creation of limited, trite, and even unrealistic plot structures. Second, Conflict is so simplistic that it does not embrace all forms of drama and literature. Third, the theory of conflict through its associations with strife presents violence as a basic element of drama and literature when this is not the case at all. Conflict theory is workable because it is an extraction of vector theory, but it fails to clearly define the workings of plot, not even giving a valid definition of the climax.

Historically, the aesthetic writings on conflict theory have ventured very close to vector theory.

Hegel's notion of 'tragic conflict' from which today's conflict theory arises is couched in terms of an "unstable equilibrium between man's will and his environment—the wills of other men, the forces of society and of nature" (Lawson, 1960, p. 37). In other words, forces are out of balance. John Howard Lawson in his much lauded book, *Theory and Technique of Playwriting*, which first came out in 1936, takes Hegel's concept of an imbalance of forces and Brunetiere's concept of struggling forces to define the climax in language akin to vector theory: "The climax resolves the conflict by a change of equilibrium which creates a new balance of forces..." (Lawson, p. 178).

Lawson's statement is reflective of vector analytical principles, but Lawson falls short of explaining how the new balance of forces is created. Lawson's (1960, p. 178) assertion that "the climax is the concrete realization of the theme in terms of an event," and that "In practical playwriting, this means that the climax is the point of reference by which the validity of every element of the structure can be determined" coincides with a vectorial analysis of literature and drama in that the elements of the structure are forces and the majority of forces converge at the climax. The resultant of the climactic convergence, the new balance of forces of which Lawson speaks, is the final expression of the theme of work as revealed by the direction of the resultant force. Each force that converges at the climax has a direction, and as has been discussed before, it is the establishment of the directions of the forces that define the theme of the piece. Thus, as Lawson says, in creating plays (and other works of drama and literature) any force that does not ultimately contribute to the formation of the specific resultant of the climactic convergence is not valid because it is through the direction of the forces and most specifically the direction of the climactic convergence's resultant force that the theme of the work is expressed. Hegel's original idea of drama being created out of the motion of forces that are in unstable equilibrium and Lawson's notion that the climax is the moment when a new balance of forces is created is in line with vector theory and free of the pitfalls to which the current version of conflict theory leads.

Two questions arise from the narrowing of the concept of conflict theory from Hegel's basically vectorial one and the current form of conflict as aggression. One question is, if Hegel's notion that it is an imbalance of forces that is the basis of plot instead of a struggle

**of wills, then has there been any trend in
fiction or drama that is concerned with
balance instead of violence?   The second
question is, why would an interpretation of
violence regarding Hegel's concept of conflict
come to be the norm for plot construction?**

Feminist theory provides a way of looking at these
questions.   The answer to the second question, via
feminist theory, is found in that aggression and fighting—
conflict—are related to the sex-role stereotype of male
aggression and dominance.   Feminist theory has
determined that "the sex-role stereotype seems to be
reasonably accurate in aggression, assertiveness, and
dominance (Bee, 1992, p. 447) and the reasons for the
aggression include such variables as higher testosterone
levels in males (Durkin, 1995, pg.   401), fatherly
punishment and prohibitions towards boys as young as
one year old (Bee, p. 447), and elementary school peer
rejection (Bee, pg. 445). In a social system in which "both
men and women are taught to equate true masculinity with
violence and dominance" (Eisler, 1987, pg. xviii) and in
which until very recently most professions were dominated
by, often exclusively reserved for men and conducted in
the "traditional 'male' hierarchical command-and-control
model" (Hales, 1999, pg.   330) it is no wonder that the
prevailing theory of plot construction is the current
aggression based form of conflict theory.
The answer to the first question—has there been any
trend in fiction or drama where plot is concerned with
balance instead of violence—is, yes, there has been such
a trend. Ironically, this trend lies in the area of fiction most
known for being written by and for men—speculative
fiction, more precisely science fiction and fantasy.   As
more women have entered the field of science fiction and
fantasy more aspects of women's points of view have

been expressed in speculative fiction. Antagonists are no longer merely villains; they are characters whose circumstances and needs are different from those of the protagonists' but are not necessarily bad. The protagonist is no longer solely an admired strong man, but a character who often has some serious personality or behavioral flaws.

For instance, in Ellen Kushner's *Thomas the Rhymer*, the Fairy Queen is not characterized as an evil temptress who tricks Thomas into becoming her slave for seven years, taking him away from the mortal woman he truly loves. The Fairy Queen is granting him something he really wishes, to be her favored courtier in the land of Fairy, and Thomas loves the Fairy Queen as much as his mortal love. Thomas comes to believe there is a battle going on in Fairy, but it turns out differently than he expects. The Fairy Queen is at odds with her own husband, and she needs Thomas's help not to overthrow or destroy her husband, but to resolve the differences that have arisen in such a way as to maintain her power while satisfying her husband's needs. The point of the climax is to avoid actual conflict while restoring harmony.

Sharon Shinn's *Archangel* also can be regarded as a plot that uses restoring balance and harmony for its shape rather than the aggression of conflict. As the blurb of the book says: "Through science, faith and force of will, the Harmonics carved out for themselves a society that they conceived of as perfect. Diverse peoples held together by respect for each other and the prospect of swift punishment if they disobey their laws. Fertile land that embraced a variety of climates and seasons. Angels to guard the mortals and mystics to guard the forbidden knowledge. Jehovah to watch over them all..."

The book begins when this structure has gone awry: a people are persecuted and even enslaved; parts of the land have sickened, providing no crops; some of the angels have actually murdered mortals. To solve these problems, the angel Gabriel, who is to become the new archangel, must find his appointed Angelica, who must be a mortal. Angels must marry only mortals—a form of balance. Together they must sing with representatives of all the peoples of the world joining in to demonstrate the harmony between everyone. Indeed most of the crucial scenes, the scenes of greatest drama, are scenes of singing. Gabriel first realizes his future Angelica, Rachel, is in the same city as he when he sings; to bring rain to a drought ravished land Gabriel sings; to prevent Jehovah from destroying the world, Gabriel and Rachel lead the singing of thousands assembled in a plain; and to bring Gabriel to her, to tell him she does love and want him, Rachel sings a song that had been lost and is fabled to entice Jehovah to rain manna upon the people. The harmony of music instead of the violence of conflict is used to construct the plot.

My novel, *Zollocco: A Novel of Another Universe*, also takes the approach of balance rather than conflict. The protagonist, a woman, has somehow been conveyed away from the dying Earth to a spaceship of another universe. She escapes the spaceship to land and dwell in a world of forests where the forests are sentient. She learns to directly communicate with animals and vegetation, and learns that it has been humanity's failure to commune properly with nature that has led the earth to the brink of death. The worlds of the universe among which she travels are also threatened by a resurgence of the same problem in the form of a corporation's attempts to enslave some people and to end the forest world's governance of the planets. The many priesthoods of the forests have not been able to curb the corporation's nefarious doings—the most powerful sect that unites the priesthoods being short of a needed member. The climax consists of the transformation of both the protagonist and the antagonist into truer versions of themselves. The antagonist becomes a raging beast, the protagonist a priestess of transcendental powers. The beast rushes off into the depths of the forests; the priestess ascends to a moon.

Although violence towards the protagonist and destruction of the earth are threatened they are staved off through replacing confrontation with self-reflection.

The current understanding of conflict theory arises from the patriarchal tendencies towards aggression and the destruction of an enemy while tales like Kushner's, Shinn's, and mine use the concept of balance or harmony needing to be established. Conflict theory follows vector theory exactly if extremely narrowly and this is why it has been such a workable theory for plot construction. Tales such as Shinn's, Kushner's, and mine that move away from the violent and hierarchal structures associated with conflict theory also follow the principles of vector theory exactly. These stories have locations, characters, and objects which are acted upon by the thematic forces of the works. Each of the characters of these books is propelled by the thematic forces to converge with other characters, objects, or locations; the convergences create rising action, and usually the key convergences are not represented as moments of aggression or violence. Just as in stories framed around conflict theory, the forces of the stories all converge at the same time and place to create a climax, but the climax is not a moment where a hierarchy is established or an enemy destroyed—the resultant transformation is to the benefit of all. In Shinn's book, manna rains down upon the world; in Kushner's the Fairy Queen and King may now harmoniously reunite; and in *Zollocco* greater power is created in both woman who is priestess and in woman who is beast. As *Archangel*, *Thomas the Rhymer*, and *Zollocco* show, well structured works of fiction need not depend on aggression and violence to form rising action and climaxes. The "traditional 'male' hierarchical command-and control model" of conflict theory and the female approach of encouraging individual growth (Hanes, 1999, pg. 330) where all benefit through restored harmony are both fully described by vector theory. Vector analysis provides a unifying theory of plot construction for male and female orientations towards storytelling.

The replacing of conflict theory with vector theory is probably the greatest contribution this book can make. I, like many people, feel that the constant barrage of violent images of which so much of film and fiction consists is not only stupid, boring, and disgusting, but is psychologically unhealthy and dangerous for the society at large, for at worst it encourages a lust for violence and gore and at best teaches that aggression is a norm to be accepted. This does not mean that all moments of violence in drama and literature need or should be eschewed, but the notion that violence as the be all and end all of plot must end.

Chapter Eight:
Examples of Vectorial Analysis of Literature

In order to demonstrate that vector theory is universally applicable, examples from different cultures and eras are given here in this chapter. Throughout this book examples from novels, plays, films, and short stories have been touched upon, giving, it is hoped, sufficient idea of the general means of analyzing works of literature and drama vectorially. Poems are chosen here for in depth, line by line analysis because poems by nature are short yet many-layered. Also, the interpretation of poetry shares with the theater's metaphorical analysis the understanding that the specific elements of a piece are symbolic of a range of associations and meanings in order to tell "many stories with one story" giving a larger picture and meaning to the story. Drawing metaphorical associations from the elements of a piece is not "reading things into it" as those not trained in the theater or humanities sometimes claim; it is the art of the reader and the actual work of the dramatic interpreter; a work so important to theater that how fully the associations are understood and manipulated makes the difference between entertainment and art.

Chosen are four poems: one, a Welsh poem from the Bardic tradition of the Brisitsh Isles, then two Asian poems, one Japanese, one Chinese, and finally a Sumerian epic. Interestingly, there are many similarities between the Welsh poem and the Japanese one. Both make use of nature to root the reader in a common experience with the speaker. Second, the images of nature, the call of a cuckoo from a grove are used in both to set the emotional tone of the poems and as the central metaphors. On first reading of the these particular poems, the Welsh one seems to have a very bitter ending, and the Japanese haiku seems a bit nebulous. Vector theory helps to bring out the subtler meanings imbued in the poems, lifting some of the bitterness of the Welsh poem and clarifying the mystery of the haiku. "To understand a good haiku one has to read it over many times" (Henderson, p. 4); indeed, this is true of all good poetry. Vector theory helps to organize one's readings allowing interpretation to take place more smoothly and systematically.

The first poem, "Sadness in Spring" (trans. Gwyn Jones, 1977) is an anonymous Welsh poem from the Bardic tradition. It is dated as being written in the sixth century CE. Although Wales is part of the British Isles, the Celtic heritage is a significantly different cultural strain than the ancient Greek and Roman cultures which were the more dominant influences of Western European intellectual culture. Although the poem shares the Christian identity of Western European culture, the approach to Christianity stems from the pre-Christian, Celtic sensibilities.

Sadness in Spring
Translated by Gwyn Jones

Maytime, loveliest season,
Loud bird-parley, new growth green,
Ploughs in furrow, oxen yoked,
Emerald sea, land-hues dappled.

When cuckoos call from fair tree-tops
Greater grows my sorrow;

Stinging smoke, grief awake,
For my kinsfolk's passing.

On hill, in vale, on ocean's isles,
Whichever way man goes,
Blest Christ there's no evading.

In the first quatrain, the beauties of a spring landscape are described. Three vectors are established: a season of new life—"new grass green"; the beautiful vigor of nature—"loud bird-parley"—"land hues dappled"; and human effort serenely controlling life—"Ploughs in furrow, oxen yoked." The second quatrain takes the elements of season, nature, and human effort and reverses them creating countering dark and mournful vectors. The call of cuckoos, for the Celts of the British Isles of Medieval and earlier times, was a mournful sound. "Stinging smoke" raises images of the smoke from chimneys, the human element in the pastoral scene, but the sting of smoke causes eyes to tear and so "grief awakes." Spring marks the passing of winter, but many a soul in the time of the poem would have passed away in the winter, and so, as spring means winter has passed so it also brings the memory of who has passed away. A vector of movement, of passage from one season to another, from one state to another, is brought into the poem by the "my kinsman's passing" line.

The final tricet brings the vectors together: "on hill" where the birds sing in the trees refers both to the beauty of spring and the mournful element represented of the cuckoo; "on vale" refers to the beauty of "land hues dappled," human labor to control nature by ploughing furrows and yoking oxen, and the Biblical line of "the valley of death"; "on ocean's isles" refers to both beauty of the sea and thoughts of escaping to or from islands. The list of places combines the vectors of beauty of nature, labor to control nature, and grief of the course of nature (towards death) with the second line of the tricet to converge with the vectors of passage: passage from place to place, and passage that is an attempted escape from death. The resultant, the last line, is powerfully transformative—"Blest Christ"; there had been only one references to religion or God until the moment of climactic convergence. The adjective "Blest" is striking, at the moment of greatest grief this word is inserted, suggesting that what lies beyond grief and death is the glory of Christ. In the falling action of the poem—"there's no evading"—it is clear that regardless of their love of nature and their efforts to control it, the speaker of the poem and his kinsman will inevitably pass from nature's realm to unite in the blessing of Christ's.

The next two poems come from Asia. The first is the Japanese poet Basho's haiku, "Bamboo Grove" written in 1691 (translated by Thomas Lipschultz, 2004), and the second is the Chinese poem, "On the Mountain: Question and Answer" by Li Po, who lived from 699 to 762 CE (Birch and Keene, 1965, p. 225).

Bamboo Grove
by Basho

Cuckoo, cuckoo's cry
Listen, Light of the full Moon
Fills the bamboo grove

Cuckoo's, as migratory birds, seek out warmer temperatures, and so as in the Welsh poem, the cuckoo is a reference to spring. "The song of *hototogisu,* the little Japanese cuckoo is usually heard at dusk. It is considered to be not only beautiful but slightly sad; other names for the *hototogius* are 'bird of the other world,' 'bird of disappointed love,' etc" (Henderson, p. 6). Thus, the cuckoo, in this poem, introduces negative vectors of mystery, death, and disappointed love as well as positive vectors of beauty and spring-time.

The second line suggests that the moon is being addressed; indeed, in the original Japanese "the intention of this sentence appears to be that of addressing the moon" (translator's note). The moon in many cultures is associated with women and so can here can be interpreted as a woman seen at dusk at an upper window or standing upon a balcony or porch. The metaphor of the moonlight suggests that her brilliance, like the full moon, is rarely seen, rarely met with. Since the woman is addressed, the cry of the cuckoo then takes on the suggestion that the woman is being serenaded with a slightly mournful song. The woman can be considered to have the qualities of a Japanese cuckoo which is a small bird. Cuckoos are timid and rarely seen and have a song of great, if mournful, beauty. That a cuckoo represents a young and delicate woman makes it a negative vector in the way that yin is negative, and her suggested beauty means she has great magnitude.

The third line, also sharing a resemblance to the Welsh poem, gives the image of "fair treetops" in that though bamboo is a grass, it is a very large tree-like grass forming groves and forests. Thus, someone is in the grove of bamboo, probably a young man—the lover of the young woman—who serenades her. The bamboo refers to the young man, a positive vector as yang is positive, just as the moon refers to the young woman. The vectors of the young woman, the young man, and the mournful song of the cuckoo converge in the final line. The light of the moon fills the bamboo grove, suggesting that the young man's thoughts are filled with the woman; indeed she fills the thoughts of all of the young men—a full grove of them. The young man has the considerable magnitude of the bamboo grove. Bamboo groves are dense; bamboo groves are beautiful; bamboo provides food, a highly valued medicine (in early times, perhaps in Basho's time), and material for building housing; all of which suggests he is well capable of providing for her as a husband. However, as he is skulking about in the foliage hoping to catch sight of her, there is again the suggestion that this is an illicit love, that he is not, for some reason, allowed to marry her as he wishes. Thus there is a negative vector suggested by the grove—the vector of trespass or hiding—and this negative vector becomes more powerful as it converges with the cuckoo's cry. The cuckoo's cry as well as the moonlight fills the grove.

The moonlight filling the grove can be interpreted as the woman herself, in her flowing white kimono, slipping through the bamboo to the young man. The mystery and sense of something amiss suggested by the metaphor of the cuckoo is deepened when it is considered that cuckoos replace other bird's eggs with their own, leaving their eggs to be hatched and the cuckoo hatchlings raised by the other birds and often fighting with its foster siblings. Is she little more than a young girl sent to court, unhappy among strangers? Is the young man thinking that she may bear his children under the pretense that they are the children of her husband? In each of these cases he would have reason to want to steal her away to his own home as Lord Genji did with many of his concubines, and so there is the echo in the poem of the *Tale of Genji*. "As would naturally be expected, many haiku evoke associations by references to Buddhist beliefs, to social customs, and to episodes in Japanese history..." (Henderson, p. 6).

The third line suggests that the young woman looks out over the bamboo, and the young man catches a glimpse of her face as though she were the moon. That the moonlight "fills" the bamboo—perhaps she comes down and runs through the trees to him—gives a sense that the bamboo is being permeated with the essence of the moon. When the moon is regarded as the woman and the bamboo as the man, the line conveys the feeling that her essence, her soul, has similarly permeated his being, filling him with her transcendent light, joining them in a deeply spiritual affinity. The mournfulness—the "other worldly" quality of the cuckoo's song—makes the reader wonder if this love between the young man and woman will end in tragedy—at the least, their never being able to be joined in this life, and at the worst, their deaths.

In this poem the few images provided are each rich with a multitude of symbolic meanings. Vector theory assists with the interpretive process in revealing the magnitude and sense of the various symbolic forces. The tragic, but lovely song and the tragic lovers converge in the second line when the man addresses the woman and climactically converge in the third line when the tragic, lovely song and the tragic, lovely woman fill the heart of the similarly lovely and tragic young man. By considering the metaphorical statements vectorially, the structuring of the metaphorical statements—the cry of the cuckoo, the addressing the moon, the moonlight filling the bamboo grove— allows the story implied by the metaphorical statements to be more quickly and fully grasped.

On the Mountain: Question and Answer
by Li Po

You ask me:
    Why do I live
on this green mountain?
    I smile
    No answer
        My heart serene
On flowing water
        peachblow
        quietly going
        far away

        another earth
This is
        another sky

No likeness
    to that human world below.

Li Po's "On the Mountain: Question and Answer" takes as its subject the convergence between three major sets of vectors and the resultant their convergence creates. One set of vectors is the pair of characters: the young man posing the question and the old man responding. The young man represents the need to attend to one's community: the old man represents the need to attend to one's individualism. The second set of vectors is that of meanings, speech and silence—the young man asks a question and the old man's response is silence. The third set of vectors is of the settings: the pristine mountain contrasting with the settled valley.

The magnitudes of the vectors are established by the relative shortness of the posed question and the relative length of the answer. The answer is the description (which takes up two-thirds of the poem) of the old man's state of mind and of the surroundings. Although the old man gives a silent reply, more words are needed to form his answer than are needed to ask the question. Magnitude is also shown in a set of levels—the lowly (those in the valley) being a weaker magnitude than the lofty (he on the mountain top).

The direction of the vectors is the same; it is the path between the earthly world and the divine—from the foot of the mountain up to its zenith and on into the heavens: "another earth/another sky." That the vectors share the same direction is made evident by the image of traveling between mountain top and valley. The young man, however, will go back down to the valley again, but the old man will be "quietly going/far away" on up to heaven. Since the young man will be traveling from the upper world to the lower, the sense of the young man is negative. The urbanized valley is also negative, for it is "that human world below," the mundane world of human concerns, but the old man's heart is "on flowing water/...quietly going" to the divine world, making the old man's sense positive.

Thus, in this poem the distinction between sense and direction can be plainly seen. The old and the young both travel along the same path (direction) between the human world and divine, but they head toward different points of termination. The resultant of the convergence of these vectors transforms them so that their true natures are revealed. Although the young man's question is accusatory, suggesting the old man is selfish and irresponsible to stay up on the mountain, this is not the case. The vectors of the mountain top, the old man, and his silence are transformed by the convergence into the powerful positive vector of the divine world. They stand revealed as positive vectors through their unity—"I smile/No answer/My heart serene/peachblow..." The images are all of serenity, beauty, and joy. The reader is elevated to that other earth and sky because the bulk of the poem has been dedicated to that resultant. The reader is caught up in the resultant's pathway, great power, and positive sense. The reader is then released from the positive resultant that is the divine world by being cautioned that it bears "No likeness to that human world below." The ending of the poem on the word "below" accomplishes closure by setting the reader back down in the human world away from the divine one. By focusing on the resultant and its transformative nature Li Po created much of the transcendental spiritual quality of his poem "On the Mountain: Question and Answer."

The next example is one of the earliest works of literature ever written: a Sumerian myth, "Inana's Descent to the Nether World" (Black, J. A., Cunningham, G., Robson, E., and Zólyomi, G, 1998)

Inana's Descent to the Nether World: Translation

1-5   From the great heaven she set her mind on the great below. From the great heaven the goddess set her mind on the great below. From the great heaven Inana set her mind on the great below. My mistress abandoned heaven, abandoned earth, and descended to the underworld. Inana abandoned heaven, abandoned earth, and descended to the underworld.

Here a very clear vector is established; the Inana

vector has great magnitude as indicated by her being a deity and being of both "great heaven" and earth (two out of three realms); the direction runs between heaven, earth, and the "great below." As the protagonist, the central character of the story, and referred to as "my mistress," the Inana vector has a positive sense. Further, the mention of Inana abandoning both heaven and earth indicates that Inana is influenced by the two vectors of heaven and earth. We can expect her, then, to act in ways that are of heaven (spirit) and to act in ways of earth (flesh). As a goddess of both, both are holy and so both are of positive sense.

6-13   She abandoned the office of en, abandoned the office of lagar, and descended to the underworld. She abandoned the E-ana in Unug, and descended to the underworld. She abandoned the E-muc-kalama in Bad-tibira, and descended to the underworld. She abandoned the Giguna in Zabalam, and descended to the underworld. She abandoned the E-cara in Adab, and descended to the underworld. She abandoned the Barag-dur-jara in Nibru, and descended to the underworld. She abandoned the Hursaj-kalama in Kic, and descended to the underworld. She abandoned the **E-Ulmac in** Agade, and descended to the underworld. (1 ms. adds 8 lines: She abandoned the Ibgal in Umma, and descended to the underworld. She abandoned the E-Dilmuna in Urim, and descended to the underworld. She abandoned the Amac-e-kug in Kisiga, and descended to the underworld. She abandoned the E-ecdam-kug in Jirsu, and descended to the underworld. She abandoned the E-sig-mece-du in Isin, and descended to the underworld. She abandoned the Anzagar in Akcak, and descended to the underworld. She abandoned the Nijin-jar-kug in Curuppag, and descended to the underworld. She abandoned the E-cag-hula in Kazallu, and descended to the underworld.)

This section emphasizes that Inana is going directly down. That she is abandoning so many people emphasizes that she is a goddess of tremendous power. She has great magnitude. This implies that when she does enter the underworld she may have enough power to escape it again.

14-19   She took the seven divine powers. She collected the divine powers and grasped them in her hand. With the good divine powers, she went on her way. She put a turban, headgear for the open country, on her head. She took a wig for her forehead. She hung small lapis-lazuli beads around her neck.

Here her magnitude is being quantified: seven divine powers and special things for her head. This suggests Inana embodies a vector of great intelligence (the turban and the wig) and perhaps another of powerful words (the necklace). The mention that the powers are "good" and the fineness of her things again emphasize that she has a positive sense.

20-25   She placed twin egg-shaped beads on her breast. She covered her body with a pala dress, the garment of ladyship. She placed mascara which is called "Let a man come, let him come" on her eyes. She pulled the pectoral which is called "Come, man, come" over her breast. She placed a golden ring on her hand. She held the lapis-lazuli measuring rod and measuring line in her hand.

This description indicates Inana also is affected by vectors of female sexuality and gender. These vectors, too, are of great of magnitude since there is power in physical beauty. It can probably be safely assumed that her beauty and the fineness of jewels indicate the female sexuality vector's sense is also positive. Therefore, this passage suggests that men will be instrumental to the issue of Inana's rescue and that there will be a lover or husband vector in the story because the positive vector of Inana's female sex must be countered by a negative vector of male sexuality and gender.

26-27   Inana traveled towards the underworld. Her minister Nincubura traveled behind her.

The story is conveying a great sense of movement with these constant reminders that Inana is going downwards. Here a new vector is introduced in the body of Nincubura.

28-31   Holy Inana said to Nincubura: "Come my faithful minister of E-ana, my minister who speaks fair words, my escort who speaks trustworthy words (1 ms. has instead: I am going to give you instructions: my instructions must be followed; I am going to say something to you: it must be observed).

This passage establishes that Nincubura represents the positive sense vectors of loyalty, obedience, and truth. The passage further emphasizes Inana's magnitude; she has the right to give orders that are obeyed completely.

32-36   "On this day I will descend to the underworld. When I have arrived in the underworld, make a lament for me on the ruin mounds. Beat the drum for me in the sanctuary. Make the rounds of the houses of the gods for me.

This passage shows Inana has an idea of the risk of her endeavor and an inkling of what may befall her. Through this the negative vector of death is being established.

37-40   "Lacerate your eyes for me, lacerate your nose for me. (1 ms. adds the line: Lacerate your ears for me, in public.) In private, lacerate your buttocks for me. Like a pauper, clothe yourself in a single garment and all alone set your foot in the E-kur, the house of Enlil.

The Nincubura vectors of loyalty, obedience, and truth are being projected so that other vectors in the form of other gods can be directed to add their magnitude to the Inanan vector.

41-47   "When you have entered the E-kur, the house of Enlil, lament before Enlil: "Father Enlil, don't let anyone kill your daughter in the underworld. Don't let your precious metal be alloyed there with the dirt of the underworld. Don't let your precious lapis lazuli be split there with the mason's stone. Don't let your boxwood be chopped up there with the carpenter's wood. Don't let young lady Inana be killed in the underworld."

Vectors can be represented in various forms; here the words that Nincubura is to speak are actually Inana's. Thus, the Nincubura vectors of loyalty, obedience, and truth will converge with the Inana vectors of seven divine powers, beauty, and powerful speech to converge with the Enlil-vector. It is not yet clear what the Enlil vector is; only that it is godly is revealed at this point.

48-56   "If Enlil does not help you in this matter, go to Urim. In the E-mud-kura at Urim, when you have entered the E-kic-nu-jal, the house of Nanna, lament before Nanna: "Father Nanna, don't let anyone kill your daughter in the underworld. Don't let your precious metal be alloyed there with the dirt of the underworld. Don't let your precious lapis lazuli be split there with the mason's stone. Don't let your boxwood be chopped up there with the carpenter's wood. Don't let young lady Inana be killed in the underworld."

This passage shows that the Enlil-vector may prove to be counter to the Inana vector, and so negative. If it is, the combined Nincubura/Inana vector must try to converge with another hoped to be positive vector, Nanna.

57-64   "And if Nanna does not help you in this matter, go to Eridug. In Eridug, when you have entered the house of Enki, lament before Enki: "Father Enki, don't let anyone kill your daughter in the underworld. Don't let your precious metal be alloyed there with the dirt of the underworld. Don't let your precious lapis lazuli be split there with the mason's stone. Don't let your boxwood be chopped up there with the carpenter's wood. Don't let young lady Inana be killed in the underworld."

This passage indicates that the Nanna-vector may also prove to be negative, but there is a final hope that the Enki-vector will be a positive vector.

65-67 "Father Enki, the lord of great wisdom, knows about the life-giving plant and the life-giving water. He is the one who will restore me to life."

Literarily, this could be considered giving the story away, or as is more emotionally true, Inana's anxious hope that Enki does have what she hopes he has and will do what she hopes he can do. The description here identifies Enki as a very powerful vector of positive sense. He encompasses three vectors: wisdom, regeneration of life (the plant), and healing/cleansing (water).

68-72 When Inana traveled on towards the underworld, her minister Nincubura traveled on behind her. She said to her minister Nincubura: "Go now, my Nincubura, and pay attention. Don't neglect the instructions I gave you."

This is a wonderful touch; Nincubura does not wish to leave the side of one close to her who is about to die. The moment emphasizes the devotion of Nincubura for Inana and so underlines the positive sense of these vectors that these characters represent as well as their powerful magnitude.

73-77 When Inana arrived at the palace Ganzer, she pushed aggressively on the door of the underworld. She shouted aggressively at the gate of the underworld: "Open up, doorman, open up. Open up, Neti, open up. I am all alone and I want to come in."

Here the convergence between the Inana vector of seven divine powers, heaven and earth, etc. and Erec-ki-gala, the vector of death begins. The door and doorman Neti are together a vector, the vector of the brink of death where one may still withdraw and live.

78-84   Neti, the chief doorman of the underworld, answered holy Inana: "Who are you?" "I am Inana going to the east." "If you are Inana going to the east, why have you traveled to the land of no return? How did you set your heart on the road whose traveler never returns?"

"Going to the east" clearly has some specific cultural meaning for the Sumerians; however, it is logical to hazard the guess that since the east is frequently associated with the dawn and spring perhaps there is the suggestion here that Inana wishes to be reborn. If so, this presents the dramatic problem of the human condition—we die, and death is final. Neti's question becomes "If you wish to be reborn why come to the realm of death where you cannot return to the living?" If the supposition that the east refers to the place to be born is correct then the myth here is suggesting that one must die before one can be reborn. Two vectors here are being considered: the vector of the finality of death and the vector of the nature of divinity which is eternal life.

85-89   Holy Inana answered him: "Because lord Gud-gal-ana, the husband of my elder sister holy Erec-ki-gala, has died; in order to have his funeral rites observed, she offers generous libations at his wake — that is the reason."

This seems to be a complete non-sequitur, an answer unrelated to the question. Yet if it is considered that

Inana-vector includes the vector of innocent youth—she is innocent of what death means—then attending a wake she might be confused by the demonstration of grief that the generous libations are. Inana would be wondering why her elder sister would be showing such huge honor to a mere memory of a person. Inana would be wondering if such grief, honor, and devotion would be shown to her if she were to die.

90-93   Neti, the chief doorman of the underworld, answered holy Inana: "Stay here, Inana. I will speak to my mistress. I will speak to my mistress Erec-ki-gala and tell her what you have said."

The promised convergence between the doorway of death and death itself means of course that a convergence between the Inana vector of earthly life and heavenly life (physical and spiritual life) and the Erec-ki-gala vector of death is distinctly possible.

94-101   Neti, the chief doorman of the underworld, entered the house of his mistress Erec-ki-gala and said: "My mistress, there is a lone girl outside. It is Inana, your sister, and she has arrived at the palace Ganzer. She pushed aggressively on the door of the underworld. She shouted aggressively at the gate of the underworld. She has abandoned E-ana and has descended to the underworld.

In this convergence between the doorway of death and of death, it is suggested that E-ana, which is the main place Inana has abandoned, gave a great deal of power to Inana when she was there for she was of that realm, and so the implication is that the Inana vector is much less powerful without the locale vector E-ana.

102-107 "She has taken the seven divine powers. She has collected the divine powers and grasped them in her hand. She has come on her way with all the good divine powers. She has put a turban, headgear for the open country, on her head. She has taken a wig for her forehead. She has hung small lapis-lazuli beads around her neck.

108-113 "She has placed twin egg-shaped beads on her breast. She has covered her body with the pala dress of ladyship. She has placed mascara which is called "Let a man come" on her eyes. She has pulled the pectoral which is called "Come, man, come" over her breast. She has placed a golden ring on her hand. She is holding the lapis-lazuli measuring rod and measuring line in her hand."

Passages 102-113 are basically a sizing up of Inana's magnitude.

114-122 When she heard this, Erec-ki-gala slapped the side of her thigh. She bit her lip and took the words to heart. She said to Neti, her chief doorman: "Come Neti, my chief doorman of the underworld, don't neglect the instructions I will give you. Let the seven gates of the underworld be bolted. Then let each door of the palace Ganzer be opened separately. As for her, after she has entered, and crouched down and had her clothes removed, they will be carried away."

Apparently Erec-ki-gala is unconcerned about Inana's powers. The Erec-ki-gala vector of death has the power to

strip the Inana vector of all magnitude.

123-128 Neti, the chief doorman of the underworld, paid attention to the instructions of his mistress. He bolted the seven gates of the underworld. Then he opened each of the doors of the palace Ganzer separately. He said to holy Inana: "Come on, Inana, and enter."

This bolting all and then opening one by one of the gates of death will have some specific meaning to the Sumerians. Even though the exact meaning of these symbols may not be known, the drama is not lost on modern readers of the suspense of Inana passing through gate after mysterious gate. The gates can be understood vectorially as measures of and further dimensions of the Erec-ki-gala vector of death.

129-133 And when Inana entered, (1 ms. adds 2 lines: the lapis-lazuli measuring rod and measuring line were removed from her hand, when she entered the first gate,) the turban, headgear for the open country, was removed from her head. "What is this?" "Be satisfied, Inana, a divine power of the underworld has been fulfilled. Inana, you must not open your mouth against the rites of the underworld."

134-138 When she entered the second gate, the small lapis-lazuli beads were removed from her neck. "What is this?" "Be satisfied, Inana, a divine power of the underworld has been fulfilled. Inana, you must not open your mouth against the rites of the underworld."

139-143 When she entered the third gate, the twin egg-shaped beads were removed from her breast. "What is this?" "Be satisfied, Jnana, a divine power of the underworld has been fulfilled. Jnana, you must not open your mouth against the rites of the underworld."

144-148 When she entered the fourth gate, the "Come, man, come" pectoral was removed from her breast. "What is this?" "Be satisfied, Jnana, a divine power of the underworld has been fulfilled. Jnana, you must not open your mouth against the rites of the underworld."

149-153 When she entered the fifth gate, the golden ring was removed from her hand. "What is this?" "Be satisfied, Jnana, a divine power of the underworld has been fulfilled. Jnana, you must not open your mouth against the rites of the underworld."

154-158 When she entered the sixth gate, the lapis-lazuli measuring rod and measuring line were removed from her hand. "What is this?" "Be satisfied, Jnana, a divine power of the underworld has been fulfilled. Jnana, you must not open your mouth against the rites of the underworld."

159-163 When she entered the seventh gate, the pala dress, the garment of ladyship, was removed from her body. "What is this?" "Be satisfied, Jnana, a divine power of the underworld has been fulfilled. Jnana, you must not open your mouth against the rites of the underworld."

Passages 129-163 build the sense of relentless power the Erec-ki-gala vector of death has by the repetition of the answer to Inana's protests. The answers also demonstrate a Sumerian notion that the realm of death has an order to it that is inviolate that even the forces of life (Inana) cannot disrupt.

164-172 After she had crouched down and had her clothes removed, they were carried away. Then she made her sister Erec-ki-gala rise from her throne, and instead she sat on her throne. The Anuna, the seven judges, rendered their decision against her. They looked at her — it was the look of death. They spoke to her — it was the speech of anger. They shouted at her — it was the shout of heavy guilt. The afflicted woman was turned into a corpse. And the corpse was hung on a hook.

By sitting on the throne, Inana is demonstrating her wish to rule the underworld in her sister's stead. However, as Inana is of earth, not just of heaven, the judges determine physical life (Inana as the vector of physical life) must die, and so Inana does, and is treated as livestock that is to be devoured is treated—she is hung on a hook for the time being.

173-175 After three days and three nights had passed, her minister Nincubura (2 mss. add 2 lines: 'her minister who speaks fair words, her escort who speaks trustworthy words') carried out the instructions of her mistress (1 ms. has instead 2 lines: did not forget her orders, she did not neglect her instructions).

The number three will also have a culturally specific meaning. The story turning to Nincubura is vectorially appropriate because Nincubura carries the vector of Inana with her, in the form of the instructions and duties that Inana gave her. Inana as vector of physical life has been destroyed, but Inana as a vector of divine life is now represented through Nincubura's actions.

176-182 She made a lament for her in her ruined (houses). She beat the drum for her in the sanctuaries. She made the rounds of the houses of the gods for her. She lacerated her eyes for her, she lacerated her nose. In private she lacerated her buttocks for her. Like a pauper, she clothed herself in a single garment, and all alone she set her foot in the E-kur, the house of Enlil.

Nincubura is mourning the death of Inana as vector of physical life and drumming for and setting out to retrieve Inana as vector of divine life.

183-189 When she had entered the E-kur, the house of Enlil, she lamented before Enlil: "Father Enlil, don't let anyone kill your daughter in the underworld. Don't let your precious metal be alloyed there with the dirt of the underworld. Don't let your precious lapis lazuli be split there with the mason's stone. Don't let your boxwood be chopped up there with the carpenter's wood. Don't let young lady Inana be killed in the underworld."

190-194 In his rage father Enlil answered Nincubura: "My daughter craved the great heaven and she craved the great below as well. Inana craved the great heaven and she craved the great below as well. The divine powers of the underworld are divine powers which should not be craved, for whoever gets them must remain in the underworld. Who, having got to that place, could then expect to come up again?"

195-203 Thus father Enlil did not help in this matter, so she went to Urim. In the E-mud-kura at Urim, when she had entered the E-kic-nu-jal, the house of Nanna, she lamented before Nanna: "Father Nanna, don't let your daughter be killed in the underworld. Don't let your precious metal be alloyed there with the dirt of the underworld. Don't let your precious lapis lazuli be split there with the mason's stone. Don't let your boxwood be chopped up there with the carpenter's wood. Don't let young lady Inana be killed in the underworld."

204-208 In his rage father Nanna answered Nincubura: "My daughter craved the great heaven and she craved the great below as well. Inana craved the great heaven and she craved the great below as well. The divine powers of the underworld are divine powers which should not be craved, for whoever gets them must remain in the underworld. Who, having got to that place, could then expect to come up again?"

209-216 Thus father Nanna did not help her in this

matter, so she went to Eridug. In Eridug, when she had entered the house of Enki, she lamented before Enki: "Father Enki, don't let anyone kill your daughter in the underworld. Don't let your precious metal be alloyed there with the dirt of the underworld. Don't let your precious lapis lazuli be split there with the mason's stone. Don't let your boxwood be chopped up there with the carpenter's wood. Don't let young lady Inana be killed in the underworld."

217-225 Father Enki answered Nincubura: "What has my daughter done? She has me worried. What has Inana done? She has me worried. What has the mistress of all the lands done? She has me worried. What has the hierodule of An done? She has me worried." (1 ms. adds 1 line: Thus father Enki helped her in this matter.) He removed some dirt from the tip of his fingernail and created the kur-jara. He removed some dirt from the tip of his other fingernail and created the gala-tura. To the kur-jara he gave the life-giving plant. To the gala-tura he gave the life-giving water.

In passages 183-225, two of three fathers, as Inana expected, do not help. Clearly there is symbolic link between Nincubura waiting three days, there being three fathers, the three items Inana took with her—the metal, the lapis, and the boxwood, and the three realms—heaven, earth, and underworld. The items that Inana took with her will have culturally specific meanings, but probably each one can be associated with each father, the metal with Enlil, lapis with Nanna, and boxwood with Enki. That two of three divine fathers are angry that Inana "craved" the underworld in addition to the realms that were already hers makes it is very clear that Inana is trying to form into a three-fold goddess. Inana is failing at her attempt to be goddess of the underworld. It then becomes significant that the third father, Enki, helps by creating little beings out of the dirt under his fingernails. Dirt has the association with the grave, the underworld where Inana is. He takes the dirt that mortals become when they die, creates special beings out of it and gives the beings a medicinal herb and life-sustaining water. The dirt, the plant, and the water indicate that Enkil is a type of farmer deity. Since we know Inana is dead, the association with Enkil is that she will come to life again as the crops do each spring under the farmer's care.

The translation's use of the word *heirodule* is interesting because it refers to a slave that serves a deity; thus, Inana is being referred to as both "the mistress of all the lands" and as a slave to a deity. Inana then represents both the deity that is served and the deity that must serve. This suggests that Inana's facing of death is a form of service. In religion, a deity facing death is a regular theme and represents the deity's greatest service to mortals. The deity's facing death represents the deity faces what mortals must as an act of compassion; it represents the larger meaning that mortals' souls return to the deity and so is an expression of promise; and in the Christian mythos the death of the deity is a sacrifice to lift the sins of mortals. So Enkil is regarding Inana's action not as greed for more power but as a heroic sacrifice.

If boxwood is to be associated with Enkil, then the significance would lie in the fact that boxwood is used (because of its fine grain) to create musical instruments and mathematical instruments especially measuring rules. Inana wears lapis, but she also carries a lapis measuring rod. The allusion to the boxwood and measuring rod would make Enkil a mathematician, one able to properly take "one's measure." This would be consistent with Enkil as a farmer because to farm one must calculate the seasons' return. Enlil and Nanna's judgment of Inana as craving power and Enkil's measure of Inana's sacrificing herself establish that there is a vector with a direction of greed/sacrifice as a significant thematic concern.

226-235 Then father Enki spoke out to the gala-tura and the kur-jara: " (1 ms. has instead the line: One of you sprinkle the life-giving plant over her, and the other the life-giving water.) Go and direct your steps to the underworld. Flit past the door like flies. Slip through the door pivots like phantoms. The mother who gave birth, Erec-ki-gala, on account of her children, is lying there. Her holy shoulders are not covered by a linen cloth. Her breasts are not full like a cagan vessel. Her nails are like a pickaxe (?) upon her. The hair on her head is bunched up as if it were leeks.

The convergence of Nincubura and Enki has as a resultant a new force of Enkil's powers. The gala-tura and the kur-jara bear powers which take the form of a medicinal herb and restoring water. More information is given here about Erec-ki-gala; she died in childbirth. Thus Erec-ki-gala also represents the vector of sacrifice, and if she is approached with that understanding Inana herself may be saved.

236-245 "When she says "Oh my heart", you are to say "You are troubled, our mistress, oh your heart". When she says "Oh my liver", you are to say "You are troubled, our mistress, oh your liver". (She will then ask:) "Who are you? Speaking to you from my heart to your heart, from my liver to your liver -- if you are gods, let me talk with you; if you are mortals, may a destiny be decreed for you." Make her swear this by heaven and earth.

1 line fragmentary

The heart and liver clearly have some significance that has to do with sincerity. It is interesting that Erec-ki-gala who is the underworld goddess is not to swear by the underworld but by heaven and earth. Since Inana is of heaven and earth, the aim is to identify Erec-ki-gala with Inana, identifying them as the same vector. By relating the two goddesses as embodying the same vectors of birth and sacrifice, it is therefore suggested that Inana was pregnant and has braved death in the way all pregnant women must.

246-253 "They will offer you a riverful of water — don't accept it. They will offer you a field with its grain — don't accept it. But say to her: "Give us the corpse hanging on the hook." (She will answer:) "That is the corpse of your queen." Say to her: "Whether it is that of our king, whether it is that of our queen, give it to us." She will give you the corpse hanging on the hook. One of you sprinkle on it the life-giving plant and the other the life-giving water. Thus let Inana arise."

In light of the previous passages that bring up the issue of mothers dying in childbirth, the corpse becomes both the dead mother and the infant baby. It is only as a vector, a representation of the force that is newly given life that the corpse can be understood to represent an infant. The statement from the underworld that it is "the corpse of your queen" echoes the announcement that a midwife would make to a king and his counselors of an infant's sex. The answer back is that whether the baby be a boy ("king") or girl ("queen") it is wanted. Newborns are necessarily cleaned and anointed with medicines. The bathing and anointing of corpses is for many cultures the symbolic preparation for the beings' new life in the realm of the spirit. The convergence of the vector of unswerving loyalty and obedience (Nincubura's and that of the magical creatures Enkil makes who obediently follow his commands), the vector of Enkil's powers, the vector of sacrifice Inana and Erec-ki-gala represent, and the vector of heavenly and divine life Inana represents create the positive resultant of Inana's rebirth.

254-262 The gala-tura and the kur-jara paid attention to the instructions of Enki. They flitted through the door like flies. They slipped through the door pivots like phantoms. The mother who gave birth, Erec-ki-gala, because of her children, was lying there. Her holy shoulders were not covered by a linen cloth. Her breasts were not full like a cagan vessel. Her nails were like a pickaxe (?) upon her. The hair on her head was bunched up as if it were leeks.

263-272 When she said "Oh my heart", they said to her "You are troubled, our mistress, oh your heart". When she said "Oh my liver", they said to her "You are troubled, our mistress, oh your liver". (Then she asked:) "Who are you? I tell you from my heart to your heart, from my liver to your liver — if you are gods, I will talk with you; if you are mortals, may a destiny be decreed for you." They made her swear this by heaven and earth. They ....

273-281 They were offered a river with its water — they did not accept it. They were offered a field with its grain —

they did not accept it. They said to her: "Give us the corpse hanging on the hook." Holy Erec-ki-gala answered the gala-tura and the kur-jara: "The corpse is that of your queen." They said to her: "Whether it is that of our king or that of our queen, give it to us." They were given the corpse hanging on the hook. One of them sprinkled on it the life-giving plant and the other the life-giving water. And thus Inana arose.

The repeating of the passage first as instruction and then again as the event emphasizes the power of this climactic convergence.

282-289 Erec-ki-gala said to the gala-tura and the kur-jara: "Bring your queen ......, your ...... has been seized." Inana, because of Enki's instructions, was about to ascend from the underworld. But as Inana was about to ascend from the underworld, the Anuna seized her: "Who has ever ascended from the underworld, has ascended unscathed from the underworld? If Inana is to ascend from the underworld, let her provide a substitute for herself."

In the falling action of a literary or dramatic work, any questions that have not been answered are addressed. This passage establishes that the resultant force of the climactic convergence has to do with a balancing of the scales of death and of further sacrifice.

290-294 So when Inana left the underworld, the one in front of her, though not a minister, held a sceptre in his hand; the one behind her, though not an escort, carried a mace at his hip, while the small demons, like a reed enclosure, and the big demons, like the reeds of a fence, restrained her on all sides.

Inana is again the vector of physical life, and as such is restrained by the vectors of mortality.

295-305 Those who accompanied her, those who accompanied Inana, know no food, know no drink, eat no flour offering and drink no libation. They accept no pleasant gifts. They never enjoy the pleasures of the marital embrace, never have any sweet children to kiss. They tear away the wife from a man's embrace. They snatch the son from a man's knee. They make the bride leave the house of her father-in-law (instead of lines 300-305, 1 ms. has 2 lines: They take the wife away from a man's embrace. They take away the child hanging on a wet-nurse's breasts). (1 ms. adds 3 lines: They crush no bitter garlic. They eat no fish, they eat no leeks. They, it was, who accompanied Inana.)

This passage defines the vector of death, its qualities and dimensions.

306-310 After Inana had ascended from the underworld, Nincubura threw herself at her feet at the door of the Ganzer. She had sat in the dust and clothed herself in a filthy garment. The demons said to holy Inana: "Inana, proceed to your city, we will take her back."

311-321 Holy Inana answered the demons: "This is my minister of fair words, my escort of trustworthy words. She did not forget my instructions. She did not neglect the orders I gave her. She made a lament for me on the ruin mounds. She beat the drum for me in the sanctuaries. She made the rounds of the gods' houses for me. She lacerated her eyes for me, lacerated her nose for me. (1 ms. adds 1 line: She lacerated her ears for me in public.) In private, she lacerated her buttocks for me. Like a pauper, she clothed herself in a single garment.

322-328 "All alone she directed her steps to the E-kur, to the house of Enlil, and to Urim, to the house of Nanna, and to Eridug, to the house of Enki. (1 ms. adds 1 line: She wept before Enki.) She brought me back to life. How could I turn her over to you? Let us go on. Let us go on to the Sig-kur-caga in Umma."

Passages 306 through 328 discuss that Nincubura has proved worthy of life through her sacrifices.

329-333 At the Sig-kur-caga in Umma, Cara, in his own city, threw himself at her feet. He had sat in the dust and dressed himself in a filthy garment. The demons said to holy Inana: "Inana, proceed to your city, we will take him back."

334-338 Holy Inana answered the demons: "Cara is my singer, my manicurist and my hairdresser. How could I turn him over to you? Let us go on. Let us go on to the E-muc-kalama in Bad-tibira."

339-343 At the E-muc-kalama in Bad-tibira, Lulal, in his own city, threw himself at her feet. He had sat in the dust and clothed himself in a filthy garment. The demons said to holy Inana: "Inana, proceed to your city, we will take him back."

344-347 Holy Inana answered the demons: "Outstanding Lulal follows me at my right and my left. How could I turn him over to you? Let us go on. Let us go on to the great apple tree in the plain of Kulaba."

Passages 329 through 343 discuss that Cara and Lulal also have proved themselves worthy of life through their devotions and sacrifice.

348-353 They followed her to the great apple tree in the plain of Kulaba. There was Dumuzid clothed in a magnificent garment and seated magnificently on a throne. The demons seized him there by his thighs. The seven of them poured the milk from his churns. The seven of them shook their heads like .... They would not let the shepherd play the pipe and flute before her (?).

354-358 She looked at him, it was the look of death. She spoke to him (?), it was the speech of anger. She shouted at him (?), it was the shout of heavy guilt: "How much longer? Take him away." Holy Inana gave Dumuzid the shepherd into their hands.

359-367 Those who had accompanied her, who had come for Dumuzid, know no food, know no drink, eat no flour offering, drink no libation. They never enjoy the pleasures of the marital embrace, never have any sweet children to kiss. They snatch the son from a man's knee. They make the bride leave the house of her father-in-law.

Passages 348 through 367 show that Dumuzid has shown no devotion, made no sacrifice to prove his worthiness to live. Although he is Inana's husband, he is selected to be her replacement in the underworld.

368-375 Dumuzid let out a wail and turned very pale. The lad raised his hands to heaven, to Utu: "Utu, you are my brother-in-law. I am your relation by marriage. I brought butter to your mother's house. I brought milk to Ningal's house. Turn my hands into snake's hands and turn my feet into snake's feet, so I can escape my demons, let them not keep hold of me."

376-383 Utu accepted his tears. (1 ms. adds 1 line: Dumuzid's demons could not keep hold of him.) Utu turned Dumuzid's hands into snake's hands. He turned his feet into snake's feet. Dumuzid escaped his demons. (1 ms. adds 1 line: Like a sajkal snake he ....) They seized ....
2 lines fragmentary
Holy Inana ...... her heart.

Passages 368 through 383 demonstrate that Dumuzid

represents a vector in his own right, the vector of family obligation and unity. Although Dumuzid escapes the demons for a time, other stories tell of his eventual capture even though his sister kept helping him to flee. The fragmentary lines in this passage are enough to show that he is seized, but his being seized to be killed by the demons grieves Inana.

384-393 Holy Inana wept bitterly for her husband.

4 lines fragmentary

She tore at her hair like esparto grass, she ripped it out like esparto grass. "You wives who lie in your men's embrace, where is my precious husband? You children who lie in your men's embrace, where is my precious child? Where is my man? Where ......? Where is my man? Where ......?"

This is another wonderful, human touch. Although Inana flew mad and chose her husband as her replacement since he did not seem to mourn her death, she now grieves at his.

394-398 A fly spoke to holy Inana: "If I show you where your man is, what will be my reward?" Holy Inana answered the fly: "If you show me where my man is, I will give you this gift: I will cover ...."

399-403 The fly helped (?) holy Inana. The young lady Inana decreed the destiny of the fly: "In the beer-house and the tavern (?), may there ...... for you. You will live (?) like the sons of the wise." Now Inana decreed this fate and thus it came to be.

Passages 394 through 398, the passages about the flies, make it clear Dumuzid is now the corpse hanging on the hook in the underworld.

404-410...... was weeping. She came up to the sister (?) and ...... by the hand: "Now, alas, my .... You for half the year and your sister for half the year: when you are demanded, on that day you will stay, when your sister is demanded, on that day you will be released." Thus holy Inana gave Dumuzid as a substitute ....

Other stories explain how Inana was able to arrange that Dumuzid and his sister would take turns serving as Inana's replacement in the underworld. The loyalty and devotion vector is still extant in the form of Dumuzid's sister who had tried to help Dumuzid avoid death, and the vector of sacrifice remains to the last as the completely innocent sister takes a turn in the underworld for Dumuzid, and Dumuzid takes his turn for Inana. The idea that life is cyclical is suggested earlier in the story through the metaphors of Enkil as farmer replanting with the dirt from his finger nails; the metaphor of the corpse of Inana as infant; and here as Inana as the vector of reincarnation represented by Dumuzid and his sister regularly going to and returning from death for Inana.

411-412 Holy Erec-ki-gala -- sweet is your praise.

It would seem odd at first reading that Erec-ki-gala who killed Inana would be the one praised, especially as the story is of Inana. However, the story is thematically about death, and the force of death is represented by Erec-ki-gala. Also the story does carry the vector of a mother's sacrifice of her own life to bring forth life--Erec-ki-gala died in labor. The doorway, the wait, followed by seven gates may refer to Inana's own pregnancy. After a month a woman knows for sure she has missed her period completely. Then, without the benefits of modern tests, she must wait a little longer to see if her belly has grown. By the time she is sure, a full two months would have passed leaving seven months to go—the seven gates. After passing through the seventh gate Inana's dress is removed and she must crouch down—the shedding of constrictive clothing and the crouching to deliver a baby. Inana sought to become ruler of the underworld as well as of heaven and earth and the story tells how she accomplishes this. Thus Inana becomes equated with the goddess of the underworld, Erec-ki-gala through the sacrifice of motherhood.

In reading haiku one must follow the important aesthetic notion that the overtones of haiku give more levels of meaning to the poem (Henderson, 1958). This is true of all poems, all literature. In theater, it is these very overtones that are sought out to give the richness of the metaphorical image which is the production concept of a play or film. Vector theory clarifies why seemingly unrelated things in a work of literature or drama can be legitimately considered the same—like the corpse as infant in "Inana's Descent to the Underworld". When the things, the bodies of a work of literature, are imbued with the same vectors, it is the vectors, not the bodies, that hold the deeper meaning of the piece. In this way, vector theory clarifies why drama and literature, in essence, speak of truths. It is the truths of the forces that are the real subjects of drama and literature. Forces of emotion, forces of society, forces of ideals, forces of nature all act upon humans and it is of these forces and how and when they act upon humans that the arts of literature and drama forcefully speak.

Vector theory illuminates literary and dramatic theory by describing exactly why and how the symbols in literary and dramatic pieces function.

Afterword

Vector theory illuminates literary and dramatic theory by describing exactly why and how the elements in literary and dramatic pieces function. The components of plot structure—opening exposition or inciting incident, rising action, complications, the climax, and the falling action are more precisely defined. The opening exposition is an explanation of what the major vectors are; the inciting incident is a convergence between different sense vectors that creates or demonstrates the imbalance of the forces of the work; the rising action consists of both same sense and different sense vectorial convergences with each convergence creating an increase of magnitude for the resulting vectors; the climax is the convergence, usually the final one, that determines what the resultant of the piece as a whole is; the falling action is expression of the resultant—the final statement of the piece in its sense, direction, and magnitude.

Symbolism and the layering of stories and themes in literature and drama become much more decipherable with the aid of vector theory. Symbols can be comprehended through the function of the symbolized object and its effect on and relation to other symbols with the determining of their sense and magnitude. The associations that can be made for the elements of a piece are the social, emotional, and ideological forces that drive the meaning of the work and so the skill of learning to make those associations can be better appreciated. Discovery of and understanding of the various themes of literary and dramatic pieces becomes a much easier task through the precise analytical tools of establishing forces' directions.

Vector analysis allows traditional means of literary and dramatic analysis to be better understood for the types of contributions they make. The sketchiness of Aristotle's notions are filled out with a more functional analysis. The tenacity of Delsarte's ideas are understood and given credence through the recognition that they were formed for a particular type of dramatic problem—the expression of forces through language—verbal, vocal, and physical—in characterization. The idealization of the human world as conceived by the neoclassicists can be saved from triteness through understanding the verisimilitudes mean each character is a symbol of a larger force and the Three Unities are likewise a symbolic streamlining of the qualities of forces in order to create the idealization that the forces of the world are narrowly quantifiable and understandable. The Well-Made Play Structure can be better understood as a workable and flexible formula that will produce a resultant as worthy as the elements that are plugged into it. The cohesion The Method gives to the actor's art with its pinpointing of moments of transformation can be better expressed with the aid of vectorial analysis, so that Method acting does not slip into the monotony of moment by moment playing that so often plagues it. Conflict theory's devolvement into an expression of aggression and hierarchal thinking becomes exposed by vectorial analysis.

In addition to these supports to critical inquiry, vector theory aids in the creation of literature and drama. An author or playwright can decide mechanically on the forces and their qualities and how often and why they will converge. Or, the author or playwright can use vector analysis as an editing tool, to step back from her or his creation to check that it does have a climax, that the elements are organic to each other, that the piece does not lag nor rush. Indeed, I have used vector theory exactly in this way. The first draft of my novel *Zollocco* did not finish the way I wanted it to and an editor pointed out it did not have a climax. So, I identified the forces of the piece and then made them all converge; the proper denouement then fell into place with the emotional tone I had been after. Vector theory helps with the speed with which creation and corrections can be made because when it is known what is to be looked for—do the all the vectors converge at the climax, do the internal convergences work to create the wanted resultants, etc.— creation and correction is much easier to do.

Drama and literature, like all of the arts, follow principles. Vector theory gives these principles; vector theory is not a set of arbitrary rules. The difference between rules and principles is that principles are inherent to organized structures and to dynamic systems while rules are arbitrarily layered onto unrelated elements to give a semblance of organization where there is none or to force a relationship between unrelated elements. Sporting events, for instance, are comprised of rules. Rules give sports a semblance of organization. To impose rules on an organized system is to run the risk of impeding the inherent organization of the system. Such impediments eventually will halt the system itself since the system's organizing principles are being interfered with. Rules stifle the changes that are supposed to be a constant of the system. As a set of principles, vector theory describes the changes and permutations that are the nature of story-telling.

I was asked, while I wrote this book, if it were true that there actually are only a few plots. In the theater there is the tongue and cheek reply that there are only three: boy gets girl; boy looses girl; boy gets girl back. The question and the joking answer hinge on the confusion between storyline and plot. If the confusion is extended from plot to story to theme, then the question is answered considering story to mean theme, then there are infinite stories— stories of success and failure, stories of hope and despair, stories of love and loss, stories of courage and fear, stories of the deep and of the frivolous, stories of the transcendent and of the mundane, stories of every emotion and every ideal held by every soul to ever have walked the earth and is ever yet to walk the earth. If the question is answered in the strictest sense of dramatic plot there is only one: the steady rise of a sloping line that peaks and then descends in a short sloping line. The truth of the matter is that the answer unites the infinity of theme with the uniqueness of that single plot. The emotions and ideals are forces that drive each other up that sloping line through the intersections of their lines of action, and when those forces converge *en masse* then the resultant of that convergence is the new force, the one that slopes down and away from what was so artfully built up.

Colorin colorado este cuento se ha acabado.

References

American Heritage College Dictionary, (1993). *The* "Conflict." Boston: Houghton Mifflin Company.

Anonymous, "Sadness in Spring." Trans. Gwyn Jones. Found in *The Oxford Book of Welsh Poetry in English* (1973). Oxford: The Oxvford University Press.

Aristotle. "The Poetics" found in Weitz, Morris (1970). *Problems in Aesthetics: An Introductory Book of Reading.* (2nd ed.) New York: Macmillan Publishing Co. Inc.

Artaud, Antonin. (1958). *The Theater and Its Double.* USA: Grove Press.

Basho "Bamboo Grove." Trans. Thomas Lipschultz, 2004

Bee, Helen. (1992). *The Developing Child.* (6th Ed.) USA: HarperCollins College Publishers.

Black, J. A., Cunningham, G., Ebeling, J., Fluckiger-Hawker, E., Robson, E., Taylor, J., and Zólyomi, G., *The Electronic Text Corpus of Sumerian Literature.* (http://www.etcslorient.ox.ak.uk/)1998--

Chen-ToTai. (1992). *Generalized Vector and Dyadic Analysis.* New York: IEEE Press.

Clay, James H. (1956). *The Problem of What is Real in the Drama: An Analysis of Ibsen's Realism and Maeterlinck's Symbolism.* (Doctorial Dissertation, University of Illinois, 1956.)

Clay, James H. and Krempel, Daniel. (1967). *The Theatrical Image.* New York: McGraw Hill.

Coward, Noel. (1967). "Noel Coward with Michael MacOwan, a postscript." In *Great Acting.* New York: Bonanza Books.

Dmytryk, Edward. (1984). *On Screen Directing.* Boston:

Focal Press.

Durking, Kevin. (1995). *Developmental Social Psychology from Infancy to Old Age.* Cambridge, MA: Blackwell Publishers.

Eisler, Riane. (1995) *The Chalice and the Blade, Our History, Our Future.* USA: HarperSanFrancisico.

Ernest, Earle. (1956). *The Kabuki Theatre.* New York: Grove Press Inc.

Evans, Edith. (1967). "Edith Evans and Michael Elliott." *In Great Acting.* New York: Bonanza Books.

"Ghosts and Gibberings" (1891) found in *Pall Mall Gazette.* LIII, April 8.

Guerin, W.L., Labor, E., Morgan, L, Reesman, J.C., Willingham, J. R. (1992). *A Handbook of Critical Approaches to Literature* (3rd ed.). Oxford: Oxford University Press

Hales, Diane. (1999). *Just Like a Woman: How Gender Science is Redefining What Makes Us Female.* USA: Bantam.

Henderson, Harold G. (1958). *An Introduction to Haiku.* New York: Doubleday Anchor Books.

Hutton, Ronald (2000). *The Triumph of the Moon: A History of Modern Pagan Witchcraft.* Oxford: The Oxford University Press.

Li Po. "On the Mountain: Question and Answer" found in Birch, Cyril 7 Keene, Donald. Editors. (1965) *Anthology of Chinese Literature from Early Times to the Fourteenth Century.* New York: Grove Press Inc.

Li Po. "OnJensen, A., & Chenoweth, H.H. (1983) *Applied Engineering Mechanics.* New York: McGraw Hill.

Lamm, Martin (1952). *Modern Drama.* Trans. Karin Elliot. Oxford, Fasil, Blackwell.

Lawson, John Howard. (1960). *Theory and Technique of Playwriting.*New York: Hill and Wang.

Mase, G. E. (1998). "Statistics" in Potter, M.C. (Ed.) *Fundamentals of Engineering* (4th ed.). Michigan: Great Lakes Press.

Pettofrezzo, A. J. (1966). *Vectors and Their Applications.*

New Jersey: Prentice-Hall.

"Sadness in Spring" Annomous. (6th CE). Trans. Gwyn Jones. Found in *The Oxford Book of Welsh Verse in English*. 1977. Oxford: Oxford University Press.

Tsudua, R., De Barry, W. T., & Keene, D. (1958). *Sources of Japanese Tradition* (vol. 1). New York: Columbia University Press.

Werner, E. S. (1893). *Delsarte System of Oratory*. New York: Edgar S. Werner.

Wilen, Lydia, & Wilen, Joan (2000) *How to Sell your Screenplay*. USA: Square One Publishers.

Glossary

antagonist: the character which opposes or thwarts the protagonist in a dramatic or literary work; the "villain." In terms of vector analysis, the primary negative vector in a literary work.

beat: (also known as a motivational unit) a term from The Method which refers to a segment of a scene when a certain means or manner of achieving an objective is followed or when a specific objective, usually related to the overall objective, is followed; in film and in theater, the pause or moment when the character makes the decision to change tactics or change objectives.

beat change: the moment when one motivational unit ends and another begins.

beat sheet: in film, a list charting a film's major plot points.

bit: "a bit of business"—a term from the theater referring to any momentary or short action developed for either of two reasons: a) it is either particularly meaningful or elicits a particular emotion in the audience; b) meaningfully and unobtrusively occupies a character who must remain on stage but who is not an active or integral part of the scene. (The first case occurs when the script is excellent; the second is developed to remedy a poor section in a less than masterful script.)

catharsis: a term used by Aristotle to refer to tragedy's creating feelings of "pity and terror" to such a degree in audiences that it effectively purges the audience of these very emotions.

character vector: a character who is a representation of a force because the character is affected by a certain force.

climax: the most exciting moment of the dramatic or literary work occurring towards the end of the work. In terms of vector analysis, the point where all the vectors of the literary or dramatic work converge that creates the resultant and resultant meaning intended by the author or playwright.

climactic convergence: the convergence which involves all of the vectors of the literary or dramatic work; the climax.

closure: a term from literary analysis referring to techniques that let the reader know the work of poetry or fiction has come to its finish; the technique of finishing a literary or dramatic work clearly and satisfyingly.

complication: to Aristotle, the section of a tragedy from the beginning to the climax; later used in literary analysis to refer to literary or dramatic moments in which "the plot thickens:" that is, a moment where a change of events occurs which adds a new element to the structure of the plot. Usually the new element causes the protagonist perplexity or difficulty. In terms of vector analysis, a convergence with a new, and often unexpected vector that is being added to the plot.

convergence: In common parlance, the act or fact of coming together from different directions; the point of convergence; a meeting point, an intersection. This word is used in lieu of the cumbersome engineering phrase "the point of intersection of the lines of action of the forces."

Delsarte System, The: a style of oratory, acting, and movement created by Francois Delsarte based on the idea that the orator's (actor's) art is scientifically chartable and catalogable.

denouement: The falling action; the part of the dramatic or literary work that occurs after the climax. In terms of vector theory, the resultant of the climactic convergence; i.e., the new force created by the convergence of all the vectors of the work.

direction: In vector theory, a quality of a vector; the course along which a force travels.

falling action: the denouement; the vector created by the climax.

grabber: a term used by dramatic artists for an inciting incident that is particularly active theatrically that "grabs" the audience's attention.

hold, a: "to hold the moment"; a moment that is held—a pause where the actor freezes for a moment either to emphasize an important moment such as the portrayal of an intense emotion or to give the audience a moment to absorb the final emotion of a scene or play as a means of closure.

inciting convergence: the inciting incident; a convergence that serves to open a literary or dramatic work; a "grabber."

inciting incident: a moment of high excitement right at the onset of a dramatic or literary work. In terms of vector analysis, an inciting convergence.

Internal conflict: in The Method, the condition of a character having emotions or motivations that are in opposition to each other; in vector theory, the condition of a character being influence by opposing sense vectors.

internal convergence: any convergence within a literary or dramatic piece which is not the final, climactic convergence.

locale vector: a setting or locale in a literary or dramatic piece that represents a force because the locale is affected by a specific force.

magnitude: in vector theory, a quality of a force or vector; any form of measure of a force or vector.

metaphorical analysis: a term being used here to refer to the form of dramatic analysis which is used to develop an organic, all-encompassing metaphorical image for the production of a script.

Method, The: an acting style prevalent in the USA, Russia, and China which is based on Constantine Stanislavski's ideas on script analysis and actor training techniques which enable to the actor to realize his or her role from the actor's own internal states and truths; i.e. the actor "finds the role within him or herself."

mie: a term from the Kabuki theater referring to a stylized form of a hold that has a known symbolic meaning in its execution; a "startling moment."

motivation: a term important to The Method referring to the reason a character has for doing what he or she does.

motivational unit: (commonly referred to as a "beat") a

term from The Method referring to the section of a scene or scenes where a specific objective or means of achieving an objective occurs.

objective: a term important to The Method referring to the goal of a character; what a character wants in any individual scene or the work as a whole.

plot points: a term from film referring to the "turning points in the action of a script. Also called *action points* or *transition points*" (Wilen and Wilen, 2000, p. 21).

primary negative vector: the most powerful negative vector; the antagonist.

primary positive vector: the most powerful positive vector; the protagonist; the central character.

protagonist: the character with whom the reader or audience primarily identifies with; the central character; the "hero"; the primary positive vector.

prop: a term from the theater (originally "property") referring to the small, hand-held objects used by actors for a production.. By extension, any small object used within a dramatic or literary piece, especially an object handled by the characters.

prop vector: a prop that is the vehicle of a force; that is any prop affected by a force or vector.

recognition, scene of: to Aristotle "a change from ignorance to knowledge" (Weitz, 1970, p. 690); later in theatrical history, a discovery of the true identity of some character whose true identity had been concealed. In terms of vector theory, a convergence which has a resultant of a better or full understanding of a character's true nature or identity.

reversal, scene of: to Aristotle, a change which brings the opposite of what is expected. In later theatrical history, switches in the fortunes of the protagonist and the antagonist. In terms of vector theory, a convergence which leads to a decrease of magnitude for either the protagonist or the antagonist.

sense: a term from mathematics referring to the positive or negative quality of a vector; that is, the positive or negative behavior of a vector or force.

subplot: storylines that are separate from the main story but follow it thematically and often intertwine with the main storyline. In terms of vector theory, different vectors parallel or even share the same direction as the primary vector; secondary vectors that move along as a second trajectory parallel to or following along the primary vector's line of action until the convergence with the primary vector.

sustained moments: a theatrical term referring to any moment, such as a character's reaction, or a "bit of business" that is lengthened for dramatic impact.

The Three Unities: rules laid down by the neoclassicist academy of France which stated that a play must have: one, Unity of Time (events within the play must take no longer than a day), two, Unity of Place (one setting), and three, Unity of Action (one story line only, no subplots).

through-line: a term from the theater referring to a line of continuity of meaning that an actor creates for his or her character. The through-line can be any thought or emotion that a character consistently holds from the beginning of the play to the end. In The Method, the through-line is usually provided by the objective. In applying vector theory to drama, the through-line would be the direction of a character vector.

tragic flaw: an unalterable personality trait of a character that is so pronounced that it leads to the character to destruction; a theory based on this idea.

vector: a term from mathematics referring to a symbolic representation of a force, used synonymously in engineering with force; thus, a synonym for a force in a literary or dramatic work.

vector analysis: a mathematical theory that studies forces and their movements, and therefore is applied to almost every area of the physical sciences and to engineering.

vector theory: another term for vector analysis.

vectorial analysis: another term for vector theory.

verisimilitude: a neoclassical concept referring to purity of characterization—for instance heroes are always heroic with no flaws; villains are always thoroughly villainous.

Well-Made Play Structure, The: a formula devised by Eugene Scribe for creating "workable" plots.

workable: a term from the theater meaning whatever dramatic device, action, bit, moment, joke, or scene which holds the audience's attention and elicits the wanted response from them.

Yugen: a term from the Noh theater referring to imbuing elements of performance with qualities of mystery and profundity.

Index

m/cf

Oestara Publishing
Presents Mabon 2004- Mabon 2005

Nonfiction:

Cartas de Sarajevo
por Joaquin-Ramón-Chordá
Joaquin Ramón-Chordá narra sus experiencias
como un especialista de las Naciones Unidas quien
tomó parte en la reconstrucción de Sarajevo. La
experiencia de Ramón-Chordá en Sarajevo movió su
espíritu en forma que se refleja en el estilo lírico de su
narrativa.

Fiction:

The Joshua Machine
by James H. Clay,
In the first half of the 1800's in Truro
Massachussetts, the mysterious John Rills built a wind
chime that he claimed would only sound in a wind
higher than a hurricane. But John's best friend Justin has
other matters on his mind, for his uncle Antrim has
stolen his ship. Besides, Justin knows that there is no
wind greater than that of a hurricane.

Mundilia por
por Joaquin Ramón-Huguet
El idealista septuagenario Javier Malco Tovar y su
señora se estrellaron en un sospechoso accidente
aeronáutico. Su señora murió, pero Javier sobrevivió.
Durante una transfusión de sangre, Javier adquirió el

virus del SIDA. Por esto, para sobrevivir, Javier se hizo congelar. Javier despertó unos setenta años en el futuro, en el mundo de sus ideales, que era un mundo unido en paz y en la dignidad humana. Siendo la primera persona que sobrevivió el congelamiento que le curo del SIDA, su descongelamiento causo un furor y una celebración a nivel mundial. Sin embargo, esta sociedad utópica estaba en peligro de ser destruida. Cuatro de los representantes de las Naciones Unidas que crearon los documentos para sellar el tratado final de la formación del nuevo orden mundial habían sido secuestrados. Javier, habiendo tenido la experiencia de ser uno de los primeros en proponer el nuevo orden mundial en una época en que ese orden solo parecía un sueno, estudio intensamente la historia de la creación de este nuevo orden mundial, y así encontró la clave de quienes eran los secuestradores. Este asalto en Mundilla era solamente el principio...

An Affection for an Unmarried Lady
by Fanny Delarose a Regency romance
Being deemed unsuitable by the father of the man she loves is only one of the problems Ann faces. Her new brother-in- law, the Earl of Corringdon, is furious with her for deflecting his advances. The Earl wishes to destroy Ann's reputation so she will have no where to go but his house and his bed...

Zollocco: A Novel of Another Universe
by Cynthia Joyce Clay
Having escaped from a dying Earth to the solar systems Imenkapur, a young woman lands on a planet governed by sentient forests. Despite becoming a priestess of the governing forests, she is hounded from planet to planet by the Toelakhan, an interplanetary

corporation always at odds with the forests' stewardship of the planets. The Toelakhan wants to profit by putting the young woman up for sale as an exotic pet.

The Romance of the Unicorn
by Cynthia Joyce Clay

Something in Elayne's refridgerator turned her pedigree Siamese cat into a troll, and Elayne's boyfried dumped her. This is why, on Halloween night, Elayne was not celebrating but washing out her fridge. The lights went out, but Elayne continued to scrub out the fridge by candlelight until.she found an entrance to a magical world of intrigue. Elayne is sent on a quest to find the Royal Talisman of Faye; she finds her true talent, friends, and love.

New Myths of the Feminine Divine
by Cynthia Joyce Clay

"Cynthia Joyce Clay has delivered a stunning arrangement of short stories that deal with problems from a woman's perspective. Written in the style of fairy tales, many of these portray a deep understanding of the need to preserve the beautiful Nature with which we've been blessed. In my personal favorite, "The Rental," a realtor has a difficult time boosting her career, until she receives her first client, who just happens to be a witch..." Lynnette Marie, author of *Midnight Whispers*.

Cynthia Joyce Clay was judged to be a computer program on Shakespeare at the First Loebner Prize Competition of The Turing Test. The Competition was filmed as part of a PBS Scientific Frontiers episode and aired internationally. Clay is the author of *Zollocco: A Novel of Another Universe* and *New Myths of the Feminine Divine*, and she was a member of The American Repertory Company. She was invited to Russia to deliver her paper, "The Application of Vector Theory to Literature and Drama" at the international conference "Languages of Science, Languages of Art." She holds a BA in theater from Brandeis University and an MFA from the University of Georgia.